Angels of Light?

by
Hobart E. Freeman

Enlarged edition — formerly entitled:
DELIVERANCE FROM OCCULT OPPRESSION AND SUBJECTION

Logos International

Plainfield, New Jersey

ANGELS OF LIGHT?

Copyright © 1969 by
LOGOS INTERNATIONAL
Plainfield, New Jersey, U.S.A.
All Rights Reserved
Printed in the United States of America

CONTENTS

CHAPTER 1
The Reality of Modern Occultism ... 1

CHAPTER 2
Cause for Oppression 19

CHAPTER 3
Evidence of Occult Oppression
and Subjection 29

CHAPTER 4
Liberation from Occult Oppression
and Subjection 73

CHAPTER 5
Demonism Today In the Light
of Scripture 103

1

THE REALITY OF MODERN OCCULTISM

Now the Spirit speaketh expressly, that in the latter times some shall depart from the faith, giving heed to seducing spirits, and doctrines of devils.

The Scriptures predict that there will be a great increase in demonic activity in the last days. Our age is characterized by an ever-increasing flood of Satanic wickedness ranging all the way from psychic afflictions to moral aberrations. This rapid expansion of the work of the kingdom of darkness, affecting and influencing the entire world, its governments, society, the Church, and the life of the believer, is clearly seen in the almost fantastic increase in crime, lust, deceit, moral depravity, suicide, war, homosexuality, fear, worry, anxiety, atheism, disease, psychic disorders, demonic oppression and possession, drug and alcohol addiction, together with the growth and intensification of spiritism, occultism, false religious cults, and the work and doctrines of seducing spirits and demons.

There has never been a time is history when the warnings against the dangers of occultism (all forms of fortunetelling; magic; spiritism; false religious cults) were more needful than the present time in which we live. Multitudes of people, Christian and non-Christian alike, find themselves suffering physical, mental, psychic and spiritual oppression, few realizing that it is because they have allowed themselves to become ensnared in the demonic web of occultism, which is under the influence and control of the powers of darkness.

Practices which were once conducted more or less surreptitiously and abhorred by the average person as witchcraft, sorcery, and spiritism are now being clothed with a cloak of respectability and popularized through religious literature, lectures, church groups, and other media such as radio and TV whereby millions are being subjected to demonstrations of the powers of darkness by such occult practices as clairvoyance, telepathy, hypnotism, fortunetelling and other forms of divination, magic, seances, and many other psychic practices and forms of extrasensory perception (ESP). Recently, no less a personage than Episcopal Bishop James A. Pike participated in a televised seance allegedly communicating with his dead son (a suicide) through a professional medium, Arthur Ford, who is also a Disciples of Christ minister! The daily lives of millions are being influenced by the horoscope, which is the ancient Babylonian pseudoscientific black art of astrology (Dan. 2:2). Now being sold everywhere and suggested as ideal gifts for children and adults are such occult games as "Ouija," "Clairvoyant," "Horoscope," "ESP," "Mystic Eye," "Kabala," and "Voodoo." As a result of its unprecedented psychic interest, the public can also purchase such occult articles as the planchette, ouija board, pendulum, horoscope charts, tarot cards for telling fortunes, crystal balls, books on ESP party games involving mind reading, hypnosis, clairvoyance, precognition, and so on, as well as other objects of the black arts.

We find that many persons in government circles—presidents, prime ministers, congressmen, senators, generals and admirals, envoys, and members of the State Department seek and welcome the counsel and advice of clairvoyants and psychic mediums such as Jeane Dixon, whose prognostications are derived from fortunetelling cards and the crystal ball, and Arthur Ford who conducts seances while in a trance. Moreover, some law enforcement agencies unhesitatingly engage the services of psychics like Peter Hurkos and G. Croiset, who use their occult psychometric and clairvoyant powers to aid in the solution of crimes. Hurkos, for example, has assisted the police on murder cases in 17 countries, including the notorious "Boston Strangler" case. Graphology, a form of fortunetelling through handwriting analysis, is now being used by many business firms who regularly consult graphologists to analyze the handwriting of prospective employees in an attempt to "read" their character, personality, and other traits, and thereby enable them to predict their potentiality and worth, or lack of it. The CIA is said to have used handwriting analysis along with other tests, as do banks, finance companies, sales firms, manufacturers, and many others.

Multitudes, including businessmen, government and religious leaders, beset with problems, fearful and confused because of the present state of the world, and concerned about the future, are seeking help and information from fortunetellers and spiritualist mediums. Countless others have been subjected to the influences and deceptions of spiritualism, assuming everything supernatural is of God, and mistaking the powers of darkness for the power of God. The gullible are naively falling victim to the fallacious reasoning that since God can heal and perform miracles, then every case of healing and everything that passes for a miracle must be from God. Since God has spoken through men by prophecy and revelation, then everyone who claims to have a prophecy or revelation from God must be accepted as a prophet and seer. Thus psychic mediums and clairvoyants are finding increasing acceptance from every quarter by the multitudes who are clamoring for their help and guidance through the operation of their alleged "gift of God." Such delusion is nothing new, for we find it recorded in the Book of Acts (8:9-11), and we are warned concerning its increase in the last days in which we now live (1 Tim. 4:1f.; 2 Tim. 3:1f.; Matt. 24:24; 2 Cor. 11:14; 2 Thess. 2:7-12). Many others are involved in one form or another of the superstitions of magic in an effort to be healed or helped by it in some way, or in order to influence others through it.

The use of LSD and other hallucinogenic drugs,

with their resultant damaging emotional, mental, and psychic effects, have become in our times a symbol of mankind's frustration with life in the present world and is an attempt to venture into the spiritual "unknown" by unauthorized means contrary to the Divine will. It is significant that the "hippies" show considerable interest in the occult; e.g., fortunetelling, telepathy, astrology, black magic, Devil worship and other forms of witchcraft.

Reports from England, Africa, France, Germany, South America, Haiti, Vietnam, Switzerland, and all over the world, including the U.S.A., reveal that occultism in all forms is rapidly on the increase. Hundreds of millions of dollars are spent annually on the so-called occult sciences. Thousands of tons of occult books and other literature find their way into homes via the newsstands and booksellers each year. Occult influence can readily be detected in many movies, plays, and stories, while such reputable magazines as the *Ladies Home Journal, Cosmopolitan, Harper's Bazaar* and *Town & Country* now contain regular monthly horoscope columns, one being written by the self-admitted sorceress, Sybil Leek, who styles herself as "the most famous witch in the world"! In the U.S.A. alone, an estimated 5000 astrologers chart the heavens for over 10 million Americans who ardently follow this ancient black art and plan their lives in harmony with the stars, while millions more have become addicted to and are influenced by the horoscope columns in over 1000 daily newspapers. The sale of horoscope magazines numbers in the millions and is increasing yearly according to reliable sources. In America, the devotees of this form of fortunetelling (astrology) are the women who outnumber the male adherents four to one.

Business Week magazine reports that "legerdemain is becoming big business" as everyone is taking a renewed interest in magic and sleight of hand deception, including doctors, dentists, psychiatrists, ministers, advertising men, and salesmen, and even manufacturers are using the magician's tricks to promote their wares. Capitalizing on the new interest in occultism, both Ralston Purina Company and Armour and Company offer magic kits as a premium. *Time* magazine reports a great upsurge in interest in the black arts with sales of occult items such as crystal balls, tarot fortunetelling cards, and ouija boards at an all time record high. In many cities such as New York one can purchase such articles of witchcraft as amulets, hexing dolls, ingredients for casting magic spells, charm powders, mystic incense, roots, herbs, charms, magic candles, love potions, and many other occult and voodoo supplies.

Books on "self-hypnosis" are becoming increasingly popular as a sort of do-it-yourself psychiatry which promises the reader that self-hypnosis can, by controlling the subconscious, "unleash explosive powers within and make life give you what you want—more money, power, prestige, martial happiness, freedom from pain and depression, put an end to fear, and conquer bad temper or change bad habits." A relatively new and somewhat popular movement known as "Concept Therapy," a form of psychic self-improvement, similar in some respects to such mental sciences as Unity and Christian Science, is being promoted as a panacea whereby one may, through mental concentration and the observance of certain "laws," actually "heal with ideas." The mails are being flooded with advertisements offering the gullible alleged occult secrets on "how to claim one's full psychic estate" by developing one's ESP powers. Others promise instruction on communication with departed loved ones and spirit "guides," on projecting one's "astral" self outside the body in order to travel anywhere at will, on the practice of metaphysical healing of the body, and such things as how to read minds, how to gain control over others by mental suggestion, how to make one irresistible to the opposite sex, and how to predict the future.

In these times of uncertainty and unrest—in an age of materialism, when even the Church has grown skeptical of the validity of the supernatural for today, multitudes are turning to the delusions of Spiritualism, or to the fortunetellers for guidance, and are seeking spiritual enlightenment and comfort, not from the Scriptures but from the literature of occultism including metaphysics, spiritism and the religious cults with their false doctrines such as Rosicrucianism, Theosophy, Christian Science, Unity, Swedenborgianism, Mormonism, Baha'ism, and so on. The present-day quest for spiritual reality and meaning in this chaotic age is reflected in the tremendous popularity of such pseudo-Christian literature as *A Gift of Prophecy: The Phenomenal Jeane Dixon* (which has sold more than 2 million copies); *A Search for the Truth* by Ruth Montgomery; *Edgar Cayce, The Sleeping Prophet* (over 6 months on coast-to-coast best-seller lists); *Nothing So Strange* (the Autobiography of Arthur Ford, the medium); *The Search for Bridey Murphy;* and many others, including all manner of metaphysical and parapsychological literature now flooding the market on ESP, telepathy, yoga, reincarnation, astrology, psychic phenomena, flying saucers (UFO), ghosts, witchcraft, black magic, communication with the dead, hypnosis, and the supernatural and paranormal in general. Psychic interest is so high that occult book clubs have been established to meet the demand.

Feeling the contemporary Church lacks the awareness of the true spiritual dimension and its power, many are seeking spiritual understanding and direction from such organizations as, for example, *Inner Peace Movement* (IPM); the *Association for Research and Enlightenment* (ARE); *Spiritual Frontiers Fellowship* (SFF); and the *Religious Research Foundation of America* (RRFA). The occult nature of these and similar organizations is seen in their stress upon psychic phenomena and experiences, clairvoyance, precognition, the development of one's powers of ESP, personal communion with the dead and spirit "guides," and many other practices similar to Spiritualism, cults, and occultism in general.

In addition, multitudes are being deluded by

the absurd and unscriptural doctrine of reincarnation, whereby one "atones" for his own sins through a cycle of rebirths, which is currently arousing unusual interest in the Western world largely as a result of renewed interest in Eastern metaphysics and the writings of such groups as the Rosicrucians and Theosophy, as well as psychics like Edgar Cayce and Grace Wittenberger, who contend that one may find the meaning and purpose of their present life on earth through so-called "life readings," or "reincarnative readings," concerning one's alleged previous lives.

An important factor in the present-day alarming upsurge of interest in psychic phenomena, ESP, clairvoyance, telepathy, hypnosis, and so on, is the work done by such organizations as the English and American Societies for Psychical Research, as well as the writings of such men as Dr. J.B. Rhine of Duke University, author of *Reach of the Mind,* who orginated the term "Extrasensory Perception" or ESP. Researchers in psychic science and parapsychology, with their discoveries of the hitherto largely unknown psychic forces present in the world, and by encouraging the development in man of the powers of clairvoyance, telepathy, hypnotism, and psychometry, are unwittingly opening wide the flood gates for satanic influence and control of the minds of men. What are erroneously thought to be psychic powers "latent" within all men, which only need developing to bring them forth, are not forces within the individual at all, but, on the contrary, the powers of clairvoyance, precognition, telepathy, and other forms of extrasensory perception, occur as a result of an invasion by insidious spiritual forces from without which move in and begin to function in and through that individual who opens himself to these dark powers by seeking psychic experiences and through his efforts to develop the powers of ESP, or through involvement in any form of occultism. Therefore, parapsychologists, under the guise of advancing psychic research and knowledge, are encouraging young and old alike to experiment in the psychic realm (in violation of the will of God and His express commands to the contrary) for the purpose of heightening their alleged subconscious powers of clairvoyance, telepathy, and so on, apparently oblivious to the dangers of emotional, psychic, and spiritual damage to those who open themselves thereby to the influence and control of the powers of darkness. Such interest in psychic experimentation has become so widespread that more and more universities are establishing parapsychological departments for psychic research, and for those who wish to test themselves personally for powers of ESP, "kits" can now be purchased by mail for such experimentation.

Occultism and the black arts in general are experiencing a phenomenal revival of interest, influencing more people today than at any time in history. One leading university, because of the great interest in the occult, recently offered among its courses of study one entitled, "Witchcraft, Magic, and Sorcery." So-called "witchcraft parties," in which a palmist, psychic, or fortuneteller is invited to enhance otherwise mediocre social gatherings, are becoming increasingly popular. Moreover, where the youth once gathered to play innocent party games, now the form of amusements, as likely as not, will consist of such bizarre pastimes as table-tipping, levitation of bodies, seances, fortunetelling, hypnotism, playing with the ouija board, and any number of other occult practices and psychic experiments.

Leading sources report that witchcraft is being openly revived in England (and elsewhere) as the nation finds itself plagued with the greatest increase in sorcery and occultism since the Middle Ages. Thousands of self-admitted witches and devotees of witchcraft meet regularly to perpetuate pagan rituals, fertility rites, and invoke and worship pagan gods (demons, cf. Deut. 32:16-17; 1 Cor. 10:20). In San Francisco, the First Satanic Church has been founded with Anton LaVey, the priest of Satan, as its founder and leader. Devil worship is actively practiced throughout the world today—Germany, Mexico, England, America, France and elsewhere. Practitioners of occultism can be found in every city of the world, offering to the gullible guidance concerning their problems, "spirit" healing, readings of their alleged "past lives," the location of lost persons and objects, predictions regarding everything from personal matters (marriage, career, love, etc.) to counsel in business affairs and communication with the dead. The powers of darkness are sweeping across the earth to deceive and destroy as

Satan knows his time in short (Rev. 12:12). False prophets are arising who give accurate predictions concerning historical events thereby deceiving many; seducing spirits speaking through false teachers and writers are leading the gullible astray with their subtle teachings of religious error (1 Tim. 4:1); psychics, who claim their "gift" is from God, are deluding multitudes, including many professing Christians, ministers, and religious leaders, who naively accept everything supernatural as divine, oblivious to the fact that Satan also can perform great signs and wonders (2 Thess. 2:9f.); and "spirit" and psychic healers, counterfeiting the gifts of the Holy Spirit are performing many miraculous cures by occult power as seen, for example, in the drugless, painless surgery performed by Tony Agpaoa, a "psychic surgeon" in the Philippines, who uses no other instruments to make incisions except his bare hands, or Harry Edwards, a "spirit" healer in England, whose spirit "guides" heal through him often without him touching the patient. Edwards, we are told, has even treated members of the royal family itself, as well as many of England's clergy.

The current widespread scientific interest in and development of psychic research, the growing acceptance of parapsychology as a science, the use of hypnotism by psychiatrists and in medical practice, and the acknowledgement of scientists of the reality of extrasensory perception as legitimate manifestations of the mind are unmistakable evidence of the success of Satan's diabolical scheme to gain access to man's spirit as a necessary step in his invasion of humanity on an undreamt-of scale, unlike anything in the history of the human race!

Furthermore, we are witnessing an increase in occult literature geared to influence business and professional men and women, which stresses that the key to success and personal achievement is through "psychic self-improvement," or by developing one's "cosmic powers," or through "tuning in on the creative intelligence of the universe," or by learning "how to make ESP work for you," and so on. Such organizations as the *Inner Peace Movement* for example, whose stated goal is to help men develop their powers of ESP, offers "a leadership training program utilizing Extra Sensory Perception" for leaders in business, industrial, professional, and academic fields in order to develop executives and supervisors in self-understanding, and to enable them to recognize and develop potentials in their employees. The growing influence of astrologists, who specialize in forecasts concerning stock market conditions, labor and management, production, taxes, and politics, as well as business and financial matters in general, is unlike anything heretofore, as countless business and professional people seek their advice and councel. Show business people, notoriously superstitious and especially addicted to astrology for guidance concerning their professional careers, may soon find that the growing numbers of businessmen who are consulting the horoscope far exceed them in both numbers and fervor.

The success of the powers of darkness in influencing religious leaders is nowhere more evident than in the contemporary liberal and neo-orthodox emphasis in the religious schools and theological seminaries. All demonic activity and influence is not to be thought of as that seen in the violent behavior of the Gadarene demoniac (Mk. 5), for Satan often works in subtle ways also, as for instance, under the guise of modern scholarship, or through the religious cults, "and no marvel; for Satan himself is transformed into an angel of light. Therefore it is no great thing if his ministers also be transformed as the ministers of righteousness" (2 Cor. 11:14-15). There is an increasing interest on the part of ministers and religious leaders in occult literature, ESP, and communication with the dead, as well as other occult practices and psychic phenomena. One might point to the *Spiritual Frontiers Fellowship,* an association of ministers and laymen interested in psychic phenomena, communication with the dead, and so on, founded by Arthur Ford, a Disciples of Christ minister and trance medium, as an example of the growing interest of ministers in the occult in America, or to the *Churches Fellowship for Psychic Studies* in England, whose membership includes many religious dignitaries interested in the relationship between extrasensory experiences and religion. The widespread influence of psychics and other occult practitioners upon government, military, and political leaders has already been shown.

Surely, there has never been a time in history

when occult involvement is more widespread with millions deluded, including many professing Christians, ministers, and religious leaders, both as to its satanic character and its resultant psychic and spiritual damage to those who participate.

IMPORTANT QUESTIONS TO CONSIDER

Have there ever been any occult contacts or involvement in your personal life or family history? Do you know what the Scriptures have to say about such involvement? Are you aware that God condemns such participation without reservation? Consider the following questions carefully, for they may well be the doorway to your deliverance from occult subjection and oppression if you have ever participated in or practiced these things.

Have you ever visited a fortuneteller who told your fortune by the use of cards, tea leaves, palm reading, and so on? Do you read or follow the horoscope? Has anyone ever hypnotized you, or have you ever practiced self-hypnosis or yoga? Have you attended a seance or spiritualist meeting at any time? Have you ever had a "life or reincarnative reading"? Have you consulted a ouija board, planchette, cards, tea leaves, crystal ball, and such like (whether "in fun," out of curiosity, or in earnest)? Have you played with the so-called "games" of an occult nature (ESP, Telepathy, Kabala, etc.)? Have you ever consulted a medium? Have you ever sought (or been subjected to as a child) healing through magic conjuration and charming (such as the removal of warts and burns, diseases treated, and so on), or through a Spiritualist, Christain Scientist, or anyone who practices "spirit-healing," psychic healing, hypnosis, metaphysical healing, use of the pendulum or trance for diagnosis, or other occult means? (Such practices are not to be confused with divine healing through faith as taught in the Scriptures.) Have you ever sought to locate missing objects or persons by consulting someone who has psychic, clairvoyant, or psychometric powers? Have you practiced table-lifting (tipping), levitation, or automatic (spirit) writing? Have you ever been given or worn an amulet, talisman, or charm for luck or protection? Have you, or has anyone for you, practiced water witching (sometimes called dowsing or divining for water, etc.) using a twig or pendulum? Do you read or possess occult or spiritualist literature, e.g., books on astrology, interpretation of dreams, metaphysics, religious cults, self-realization, fortunetelling, magic, ESP, clairvoyance, psychic phenomena, and especially such occult magical books as *Secrets of the Psalms,* and the diabolical so-called *Sixth and Seventh Books of Moses?* Have you experimented with or practiced ESP or telepathy? Have you used the psychedelic drug, LSD? Have you ever practiced any form of magic charming or ritual? Do you possess any occult or pagan religious objects, relics, or artifacts, which may have been used in pagan temples and religious rites, or in the practice of sorcery, magic, divination, or spiritualism? Have you ever attended such meetings as those conducted by the Rosicrucians, Spiritualists, Mormons, Christian Scientists, Baha'i, Theosophy, Unity, Inner Peace Movement, Spiritual Frontiers Fellowship, Association for Research and Enlightenment, Religious Research Foundation of America, Jehovah's Witnesses, Unitarian, or others of an occult nature? Have you had your handwriting analyzed, practiced mental suggestion, cast a magic spell, or sought psychic experiences?

Did you know that all these practices, as well as any participation in them, are condemned by God in the Scriptures? Did you know that divination (fortunetelling), magic practices, false religious cults, and spiritism in all forms are an abomination to God and are under His curse? Did you realize that anyone who has ever practiced or participated in any form of occultism (whether done innocently or not) has opened the door to oppression from the powers of darkness, even though such occult contacts may have occured before one became a Christian? Do you realize that you may now be the victim of demonic subjection or oppression because of this, although you have been unaware of the source and cause of your problems? That there is a direct connection between occult involvement and physical, psychic, mental, and spiritual oppression is shown in the study which follows. We urge you to give careful attention as you read, for many have found the way of liberation when shown the occult cause for their oppression.

2

CAUSE FOR OPPRESSION

Without exception, those who have become involved in any form of occultism will eventually suffer satanic oppression in some manner. There are valid reasons for such a conclusion based both upon Scripture and experience.

1. *Occult involvement is in disobedience to God's Word and is an abomination to Him.*

All forms of fortunetelling, spiritism, magic practices, and involvement in false religious cults are absolutely forbidden by Scripture. Both their practice and participation in them are condemned by God. In Deuteronomy 18:9f., God warns:

> ... *thou shalt not learn to do after the abominations of those nations. There shall not be found with thee any one ... that useth divination (fortuneteller), or an ob-*

> *server of times (soothsayer), or an enchanter (magician), or a witch (sorceress), or a charmer (hypnotist), or a consulter with familiar spirits (medium possessed with a spirit or "guide"), or a wizard (clairvoyant or psychic), or a necromancer (medium who consults the dead). For ALL that do these things ARE AN ABOMINATION UNTO THE LORD!*

This passage sets forth the methods by which the heathen sought to unveil hidden knowledge, ascertain future events, uncover secret wisdom, and exercise supernatural powers. In contrast to the methods employed by the heathen nations for discovering the will of their gods and uncovering the hidden secrets of the spiritual realm, God declares in verses 15-22 that Israel would learn the things that she needed to know concerning the future and His will for her, not by *discovery* through the methods of divination and occult practices, but by *revelation*. The means of revelation, which would come unsought and at the sovereign discretion of the Lord, was to be through the word of His prophets (note verses 14-15). Thus, we are forbidden in Scripture to seek information or guidance from these unauthorized and unscriptural sources, and the believer who needs wisdom and guidance is admonished *to ask of God* (Jam. 1:5), for the secret things belong unto Him (Deut. 29:29).

The modern-day fortuneteller, medium, astrologer, clairvoyant, hypnotist, magician, ventriloquist, water dowser, occult and magic healer, sorcerer, conjurer, psychic, and such like, all had their ancient heathen counterpart in the necromancer, consulter of the spirits, wizard, charmer, magician, soothsayer, diviner, enchanter, sorcerer, sorceress, and so on. Man has always been intrigued with the idea of uncovering hidden knowledge which belongs only to God (cf. Gen. 3:1f.), or with learning one's fate, determining the course of the future, obtaining supernatural guidance, and various favors and powers from the realm of the spirits. Satan has always accommodated such seekers with substitutes for truth and counterfeits for genuine revelation, thus deceiving the gullible who believe that such information or help comes from God or the spirits of the departed (who are impersonated by demonic spirits). These practices are all alike condemned by God without reservation. (Carefully examine, for example, the following Scriptures: Deut. 18:9-14; Ex. 7:11-12; 2 Tim. 3:8; Ex. 22:18; Lev. 19:26, 31; 20:6, 27; 1 Chron. 10:13-14; 2 Kgs. 21:5-6; Isa. 2:6; 8-19; Jer. 27:9-10; Zech. 10:2; Mal. 3:5; Acts 8:9f.; 16:16f.; 19:19; Gal. 5:16-21; Rev. 21:8; 22:15.)

The Scriptures clearly condemn all forms of occultism as sorcery and declare that "... they which do such things shall not inherit the kingdom of God" (Gal. 5:19-21), nor enter into God's presence (Rev. 22:14-15), but "... shall have their part in the lake which burneth with fire and brimstone" (Rev. 21:8). God not only forbade participation in all forms of occultism as spiritually defiling (Lev. 19:31), but made such disobedience as punishable by death (Ex. 22:18; Lev. 20:27), and sufficient grounds for rejection of that soul by God (Lev. 20:6), for those who defiled themselves in this manner by consulting evil spirits were an abomination unto the Lord (Deut. 18:9-12).

2. *Occult involvement breaks the First Commandment and invokes God's curse.*

> *Thou shalt have no other gods before me . . . for I the Lord they God am a jealous God, visiting the iniquity of the fathers upon the children unto the third and fourth generation . . . (Ex. 20:3,5).*

Although there are few people who have seriously considered the fact, it is true, nevertheless, that there are but two sources of hidden information (whether past, present, or future), supernatural help, power, guidance, or healing—God or Satan. When one visits a fortuneteller, obviously this individual is not seeking help from God through Jesus Christ, or he would pray directly to God, or seek help through a Christian friend or minister. The fortuneteller certainly does not call upon God for the desired information, but divines by means of occult methods and demonic power, as is seen in the case of the girl in Acts 16 who had a "spirit of divination." The powers of darkness control all the various forms of fortunetelling, such as astrology, card reading, divining by tea leaves, the ouija board, palmistry, the crystal ball, psychometry, divining rod, pendulum, planchette, or in the exercise of such occult powers as ESP, telepathy, and so on.

This is also true of all forms of magic and magical rites (whether black or white magic), such as magic charming or conjuring, magic cures for either humans or animals, casting spells, mental suggestion or remote influence (in the form of suggestions given to the subconscious mind of a person by another individual), blood pacts, enchantments, amulets, and hypnosis (magic or medical).

The various forms and practices of spiritism are likewise under the influence and control of the powers of darkness, such as seances, communication with the dead (which are in reality demons impersonating the dead), spiritualist meetings, and such psychic and spiritistic phenomena as automatic or spirit writing, table-lifting, levitation, floating trumpets and disembodied voices, telekinesis, apports, materializations, apparitions of the dead, astral projections, the mediumistic trance, and many other occult practices.

There are two sources or doors open to one who seeks guidance, information which is unrevealed, spiritual or supernatural aid, or miraculous healing. One may, through prayer in Jesus' Name, seek such help from God. But there is another way to bridge the chasm between this world and the spiritual dimension—occultism. Behind the other door stands Satan and the powers of darkness who work through the media of fortunetelling, magic, spiritism, and the false religious cults. The Scriptures forbid man to seek contact with or help through these sources, for it is tantamount to calling upon another god! Satan, as a matter of fact, is called the "god of this world" (2 Cor. 4:4). It should be obvious that if one does not call upon God, through the Name of Jesus Christ, for his needs, but resorts to the occult, then there is but one other source of supernatural power which can answer him.

Did the fortunetellers pray in Jesus' Name for their hidden knowledge which they gave to you? When you inquired of the ouija board did you ask God, through Christ, for the information? Have you ever inquired of the ouija board the "source" of its information? Some who have were startled when it gave in reply "the god of Hell," "Hell," "Satan" or the "Devil"! When you allowed yourself to be hypnotized to whom did you surrender your will—to God or to some unknown power operating through the person to whom you submitted? Did you know that demons have admitted that the source of power behind the hypnotist is Satan? By what power are persons healed when it is accomplished through Christian Science, Concept Therapy, Spiritualism, magic charming or ritual, or other occult means, instead of through prayer in Jesus' Name as the Scriptures require? What is the source of the power that causes tables to lift off the floor, objects to appear out of nowhere, furniture to move or float about the room, apparitions to appear, and voices to speak, alleging to be from the dead? What strange power causes the pencil to move in automatic or spirit writing, or the twig to bend in the hands of a water dowser? Is it of God? If so, then why is it not done in the Name of Christ? What then is its source? What really is the power which enables some persons to have extra sensory perception, powers of telepathy, clairvoyance, and other psychic manifestations? Why is it some persons after a visit to a fortune-teller or involvement in some form of occultism suddenly discover that they are psychic? Why are some people able to be conscious of an event before it occurs, hear strange spirit voices, see apparitions, read the thoughts of another, and so on? Do you realize such people invariably have had occult contacts, or that some form of occultism can be found in their family history, and that the source of their psychic powers and experiences is demonic and results from opening the door to the powers of darkness through such occult involvement?

When one calls upon these forbidden sources, although Satan often accommodates the seeker with hidden knowledge or help, nevertheless, one thereby has opened the door to the Enemy who moves in and oppresses him physically, mentally, psychically, or spiritually, for the powers of darkness always exact a heavy price for their services. For instance, in exchange for information concerning one's future, psychic disturbances often result. The consequence of the healing of a burn by magic charming has often resulted in more serious physical oppression later. Participation at a seance opened the door to divisive spirits that spelled ruin to a marriage. Attendance at Spiritualist meetings resulted in severe melancholia and depression for many years. The same result followed the practice of table-tipping in another case. Commitment to a mental institution was the reward from Satan to another who had sought (unknowingly) his help from a fortuneteller. Involvement in astrology and healing through a Christian Science practitioner resulted in chronic illness later to another victim of Satan's deception, the individual also suffering spiritual and mental anguish. Many other examples could be cited, some of which will be noted later, clearly proving the insidious nature of occultism in all its forms. The "cloven hoof" will invariably be manifested sooner or later in the life of that individual who has opened himself to the powers of darkness.

All forms of fortunetelling, magical practice, spiritism, and unscriptural cultism are an abomination to God. The seriousness of this offense can be seen in no unmistakable terms in the case of King Saul who fell under God's curse, was rejected as ruler of Israel, and put to death by Divine decree because he attended a seance and sought help from a spiritualist medium!

> *So Saul died for his transgression which he commited against the Lord, even against the word of the Lord, which he kept not, and also for asking counsel of one that had a familiar spirit (a medium), to enquire of it; and enquired not of the Lord: Therefore he*

> *slew him, and turned the kingdom unto David the son of Jesse (1 Chron. 10:13-14).*

This seance, held in disobedience to God's will, is recorded in 1 Samuel 28. Spiritualists, in an attempt to justify their practice of alleged communication with the dead, often appeal to this passage in the Book of Samuel as a instance in Scripture in which a king sought information from the realm of departed spirits through a medium. However, either they are unaware of, or conveniently ignore, the passage just cited in 1 Chronicles 10:13-14, which condemned Saul's sin of seeking help by occult means from the discarnate spirit realm instead of enquiring from the Lord. Moreover, 1 Samuel 28:15-16 indicates that Samuel also disapproved of Saul's sin of disobedience by seeking to communicate with the dead through a medium.

God's prohibitions against occultism are still in effect today, for we have found in our experience in dealing with many people concerning occult oppression that those who disobey His commandments against this sin invariably fall under His curse, suffering some form of psychic, mental, physical, or spiritual oppression or enslavement, from which liberation is needed. Moreover, it is an established fact that those who have participated in occultism or had contacts with such have not only suffered oppression themselves, but often their children and descendants have fallen under the curse, for God declares ". . . I the Lord they God am a jealous God visiting the iniquity of the fathers upon the children unto the third and fourth generation" (Ex. 20:5). Many times clairvoyance and other psychic powers appear as a consequence of occult involvement, usually in the second and third generation. Edgar Cayce, for example, whose grandfather was a water dowser, gave evidence of occult subjection at an early age, relating various psychic and clairvoyant experiences. Strong mediums usually develop in this manner, as a result of what might be termed "psychic heredity." Personality and character defects, as a consequence of occult sins by one's parents or grandparents, are often seen in their descendants in the form of morbid depression, violent temper, irresponsibility, immorality, chronic fear, hysteria, agnosticism and atheism, hate, persistent illness, unpredictable behavior, and many other abnormalities. Thus, the cause for occult oppression or subjection is in consequence of disobedience to God's Word and is a violation of the First Commandment. The seriousness of this sin cannot be overemphasized and should be dealt with without delay in the manner shown in chapter four by anyone guilty of occult involvement in any form, regardless of when it occurred.

3

EVIDENCE OF OCCULT OPPRESSION AND SUBJECTION

We must distinguish between general oppression and occult oppression and subjection. Although the symptoms in many respects may be similar, in several important aspects they are not, but are decidedly the mark of occult involvement and are easily distinguished as such to one experienced in this particular area of deliverance. Moreover, liberation from occult oppression or subjection requires proper understanding of its peculiar nature and cause, the specific method of deliverance required, as well as the consequent spiritual responsibilities of the oppressed individual after receiving deliverance. Failure to distinguish between occult oppression and general demonic oppression issuing from other causes has resulted in many who have had prayer for deliverance not being set free, or not permanently liberated, inasmuch as those who have been involved in occultism have opened a "door" of access to oppressing spirits which they themselves must close by positive action and faith on their part as will be seen.

General oppression, whether mental, physical, or spiritual, may result from any one of several causes. For example, it may result from some traumatic experience, sin, weakness, emotional crisis, resentment, hate, pride, fear, or illness, as well as other causes. Occult oppression and subjection, however, always results from *an individual's involvement in some form of fortunetelling, magic practice, spiritism, or false religious cults,* either as a practitioner, or, as is most often the case, as a subject, follower, or participant.

Moreover, it is possible, as experience has shown, for some persons to be "passively" subjected or oppressed, even though they have never actively participated in occultism. The Biblical basis for this fact is Exodus 20:3-6, the "curse" falling upon "the children unto the third and fourth generation" of those who violate God's commandment by calling upon other gods (demonic spirits and powers) through involvement in occultism, seeking thereby to break through the bonds which God has set for man. The magnitude of the sin of occult involvement, which is an abomination to God (Deut. 18:12), is confirmed by its deep power of enslavement, not only upon the participants themselves, but even upon their descendants. The reality of such passive oppression and subjection will be shown in the final chapter.

Both from the Scriptures and experience, it is evident that evil spirits who oppress their human victims are of various kinds, and work in a variety of ways. There are blind spirits, deaf spirits, epileptic spirits, deceiving spirits, lying spirits, spirits of pride, intellectualism, lust, infirmity, insanity, homosexuality, suicide, fear, apathy, anger, discord, strife, hate, resentment, depression, stubbornness, misunderstanding, gossip, obscenity, and many others. Oppression may be subjective, such as insanity, lust, or loss of health through disease and affliction, or objective, in which case the victim may be plagued by demonic apparitions and voices, or troubled by discord and strife through vexation by evil spirits.

These malevolent spirits are definite personalities, not mere habits, diseases, psychological conditions, or states of the mind. Just as human beings vary in personality, power, ability, appetites, intelligence, and purpose, so do the demonic spirits. Their primary intention, as disembodied spirits, is to oppress or possess a person congenial to their particular nature or appetites, in order to hide, as it were, behind these traits, habits, weaknesses, and mental or physical conditions, and thereby escape detection. An individual given to sexual looseness and excess, for instance, opens the door to demonic control in this particular area of his life by a spirit of lust with this characteristic appetite. The same would be true concerning a person who has a violent temper which he does not bring under control, or those who are given to pride, jealousy, hate, depression, gluttony, drug addiction, or any other weakness of character, mind or body. The demonic spirits seek to oppress those whose make-up, character, temperament, appetites, and moral, mental, or physical weaknesses are most harmonious to themselves. They bury themselves in the very structure of the person and actually identify with the personality of the victim insofar as possible. This is why it is difficult for the novice to discern, or the medical doctor, psychologist, and psychiatrist to admit, the reality and activity of demonic spirits in such victims, the latter reducing such diseases as epilepsy, cancer, blindness and deafness, as well as abnormal personality and behavior problems, to functional or organic disorders. Hence, often the presence and activity of demonic spirits in their victims are described by other terms such as: complexes, habits, drives, hallucinations, delusions, delirium tremens, insanity, epilepsy, melancholia, masochism, homosexuality, schizophrenia, mania, depression, psychoneurosis, psychosis, compulsions, drug addiction, disease, and so on. It is not that the terms are entirely inaccurate in many cases, but that they are frequently inadequate in that they do not go deeply enough in their analysis of the conditions and phenomena in connection with the work of the powers of darkness in the lives of the oppressed.

Likewise, the parapsychologist describes the various manifestations of demonic powers by such terms as clairvoyance, telepathy, extrasensory perception, eidetic imagery, hypnotic suggestion, precognition, telesthesia, psychic phenomena, and so forth, holding that such paranormal abilities and powers are but manifestations and projections of the human subconscious or psyche or that they can be explained in some other natural and rational manner as a rule. Thus, we see that the presence and activity of such personal entities as demonic spirits are not easily perceptible to the analytical investigators of the paranormal, for the precise reason that Satan does not publically announce his presence and work in an individual by handing out "calling cards"!

However, there is a growing awareness among psychologists, psychiatrists, and physicians in many instances that demonic oppression can no longer be dismissed as mere religious delusion or pagan superstition, but hat it is a dreadful reality, inasmuch as there are definite limits beyond which medicine and psychiatry cannot penetrate and bring the necessary liberation to the suffering individual. In one instance, for example, the Church of which the writer is pastor was contacted by a Christian psychologist asking for prayer for the deliverance of one of his patients whom he recognized to be bound and oppressed by Satan and whom he himself was unable to help, in this instance, with mere technical knowledge and skills. After the Church prayed in faith for her liberation in the Name of Christ, the psychologist reported that she had been set free and that he was now able to counsel effectively with her, something that he had tried unsuccessfully to do previously. Dr. William S. Reed, a well known surgeon in this country, has been reported as saying in this connection that he, as a surgeon, is convinced that many psychological and physical illnesses are the result of demonic attacks upon the individual, and that he himself, on the basis of Mark 16:17, has used exorcism or the casting out of evil spirits when guided to do so, and that we should seriously consider the ministry of exorcism in modern medicine and psychiatry.

The connections between occult involvement and the oppression which results, which sometimes are clearly obvious, as, for example, in the severe psychic disturbances which followed a certain woman's participation in a seance, are, nevertheless, many times so subtle and unobtrusive that most people have no conception whatever of this insidious relationship until it is pointed out. Who would have connected, for instance, the chronic physical illness of Mrs. L. with her visit to a fortuneteller? Mr. R. did not believe that his playing with the ouija board had any adverse spiritual effects upon him until it was manifested in his inability to exercise faith to receive the Holy Spirit. For many years Mrs. T. was unaware that her persistent marital problems and apathy toward life began the day after her participation in a seance. Who would have made an association between the chronic phobias and doubts of another person and their healing as an infant by an occult or magic healer? Mr. B. regularly visited fortunetellers, but did not realize until it was shown him that this explained the reason for an uncontrollable spirit of lust, from which he could not escape, as well as being the reason for his pride, indifference, immaturity, and hate. A brutal, demon possessed child, who was subject to periods of violent rage, was the result of the parents' occult participation, but this was unknown until counselling revealed the cause. Mrs. C. suffered severe depression and had thoughts of self-destruction, little realizing that her participation in seances was the cause. Miss W. had been committed to a mental institution at one time, spent much money visiting doctors, psychologists, and psychiatrists, had sought help and counselling from many sources concerning her psychotic condition, all to no avail, little realizing that it resulted from her past fortune-telling practices and other occult connections. Likewise, Mrs. G. was unaware that her visits to the fortunetellers were responsible for the "voices" she heard and demonic apparitions she saw until this was shown her in counselling. Who would have made a connection between the morbid depression and extreme negativism of Mr. V. and his visits to Spiritualists' meetings and those of some of the religious cults such as Theosophy and Rosicrucians, even though merely done out of curiosity? Fear of crowds and homosexuality were the result of another's involvement in the practice of table-tipping and consulting the ouija board as a child. The rapid mental and physical deterioration of another victim of occult oppression was traced to submission to hypnotism and treatment by "Concept Therapy." Mrs. D. found through counselling that her depression and lack of desire for spiritual things followed her visit to a fortuneteller. Mr. T., although he had trained for the ministry, later fell back into the world, was divorced, and lost interest in Christianity, and was surprised to learn that his troubles stemmed from his practice of self-hypnosis, astrology, and other occult interests. The removal of warts by magic charming and involvement in other magic practices has resulted in alcoholism, oppression by sex spirits, and other forms of demonic oppression in some cases. The parents' participation in occult practices resulted in a young man and young woman being oppressed by demonic apparitions and vexed with other problems. Palm reading was the cause of one woman's serious domestic problems, and another's oppression in which she heard voices and saw a ghostly apparition. Water dowsing explained the resistance of one man to the Scriptural teaching concerning the Holy Spirit. It was also the cause of another's vexation with a serious problem over which he could not achieve victory, and resulted in insanity to still another who practiced this ancient heathen method of divining. Playing with the ouija board and visits to fortunetellers were the cause of Mrs. F. attempting suicide. The consequence of having a burn "blown" away by magic charming was severe depression for Mrs. R. The relation between the mental illness of Mrs. A. and her practice of table-tipping as a child seemed remote until she experienced immediate liberation upon confession of this occult sin and prayer for deliverance. Another, who could have no assurance of salvation due to a deceiving spirit who oppressed her, was delivered when the connection between her mental suffering and her healing by an occult healer (a psychometric healer who diagnosed illness by touch) was shown. Chronic asthma was the consequence of involvement in magical practices, from which a sufferer for many years was set free upon learning of the cause. Liberation from severe mental, physical, and spiritual oppression came to another who fell victim to the insidious powers of darkness after visits to Spiritualists' meetings, while another was set free from psychic subjection, which resulted from occult practices, when shown the source and nature of her extrasensory powers.

The examples from our files could be multiplied, for there are few families in which at least one member has not had contact with occult spirits in one form or another with its resultant oppression or subjection. Although few people are aware of the various forms in which occult oppression and subjection express themselves, there is no question but that such is always the consequence of occult involvement. The basis for such a conclusion can be seen in the fact that upon establishing such a connection during counselling with an oppressed individual, confession of occult sins and prayer always bring deliverance, and in instances where the individual was also psychically subjected (having extrasensory powers, seeing apparitions, hearing spirit voices, and so on), these experiences immediately ceased, proving, thereby, their occult source.

A distinction should be made between occult "subjection" and "oppression." *Subjection,* resulting from occult involvement, means that one or more of these malevolent spirits have brought the victim under the domination and control of the powers of darkness to such an extent that the individual has been made subject to, or enslaved by, such things as, for example, sexual lust, violent temper, drugs, uncontrollable thoughts, resistance to divine things, compulsive behavior, lying, hate, religious delusions, self-pity, or forms of occultism themselves. In persons so subjected, it is often found that they have become psychic themselves, and are so enslaved by occultism that often they lack the will, and sometimes even the desire, to be set free.

Oppression, resulting from occult involvement, means that one or more of these spirits are afflicting the victim with any of many forms of mental, physical, emotional, or psychic ailments and distresses, such as depression, fear, mental illness, disease, pain, apathy, marital discord, compulsive thoughts of suicide, apparitions, and so forth.

The following characteristics are evidences of occult subjection and oppression, although some of these symptoms may stem from other causes. Usually, when one or more of these manifestations are present, it is an indication of the presence and activity of demonic spirits, as well as a sign of the need for deliverance. Occult subjection and oppression may be classified for clarification into five categories: Mental and Emotional; Psychic; Spiritual; Physical; Material, Domestic and Social.

1. *Mental and Emotional Disturbances and Abnormalities.*

There are many forms of psychoneuroses, psychoses, and other mental and emotional abnormalities which have no functional or organic basis as is commonly supposed, but result from occult involvement. While it is recognized that some of the following symptoms could also be classified as "psychic" disturbances or abnormalities in character, we are intentionally limiting the forms of "psychic" subjection and oppression to the parapsychological meaning of the term; namely, to extrasensory functioning, such as clairvoyance, telepathy, precognition, and so forth, and to such psychic phenomena as, for example, apparitions or poltergeist activity, which will be discussed later. It should also be understood that many of the following mental and emotional disturbances and abnormalities often affect the behavior of the oppressed individual as well.

1. *Psychoses indicative of occult oppression or subjection.*

The symptoms that will be found in this category are such things as serious, prolonged depression or melancholia; resignation to failure or misfortune; habitual gloominess, morbidity and negativism; boredom and indifference (ennui), as well as apathy in general.

Such persons often are more interested in their own inward thoughts than in what goes on around them and often respond in an abnormal, dull manner to others and to reality. They manifest extreme introversion, that is, living within themselves and taking no interest in their surroundings. At times they shun others, often withdrawing and spending long periods alone, sometimes in a darkened room with the shades drawn in a morose state of mind. Excessive weeping may also accompany this condition, as well as self-accusation of sins, frequently with thoughts of self-destruction. Such individuals often seem to lack normal emotional response and contact with reality, living, as it were, in a private world where little affects them except their own fantasies and dreams.

Sometimes this depressive state alternates in some oppressed persons with a directly opposite mood of extreme joy, happiness, exhilaration, and an optomistic outlook (a condition known as manic-depressive psychosis). This mental disorder is characterized by extreme, sudden changes in mood, fluctuating up and down, often without warning.

Delusions and so-called hallucinations (often psychic oppression) are frequently present in psychotics who are victims of occult involvement. There may be compulsive thoughts of violence and aggression, as well as the presence of destructive emotions of hate, rage, resentment, jealousy, suspicion, envy, malice and other antisocial abnormalities. At times there is great excitement and perturbation, often over trivial matters, as well as other mania indications. Unpredictable impulses, moods, and actions characterize such an individual, as well as certain other psychopathic tendencies and behavior indicative of forms of insanity.

There is often found in such persons a continual "flight of ideas," the individual going off on one tangent or another, often without completion of a thought, in addition to general incoherence of thoughts and ideas. Generally, they are irresponsible, unpredictable, and undependable. Unreasonable attitudes or demands are characteristic of demonic activity in such persons.

As a result of occult involvement, some individuals are in subjection to extreme and uncontrollable passions and appetites. Vile language, sexual allusions or displays are common. Frequently, there may be inexplicable character or personality changes toward moral degeneracy. There may be found such sexual aberrations as: homosexuality; masochism; self-abuse; promiscuity; sadism, abnormal sexuality; uncontrollable lustful thoughts and images, as well as suggestive behavior and dress.

Also indicative of the presence and activity of demonic powers is enslavement by such habits as drug addiction, gluttony (compulsive eating), addiction to alcohol or tobacco, compulsive gambling, and many other forms of excess and intemperance.

2. *Psychoneuroses indicative of occult oppression and subjection.*

The neurotic exhibits symptoms such as persistent, chronic fear or dread. Generally, there is a condition of morbid anxiety that something dreadful is about to happen, or that one has not done something he ought to have done, or has done something that he should not have done, and so on. There are often feelings of apprehension, consternation, panic and hysteria, or evidence of strong nervous tension, the individual often working and living at a frenzied pace, and frequently suffering insomnia and extreme restlessness.

Other abnormalities are seen in neurotics such as difficulty in making decisions, inability to adjust normally to certain situations, and the need of constant guidance and reassurance by others because of personal feelings of inadequacy and immaturity, or the fear of failure. Extreme hypersensitivity, irritability, and impatience are common. The individual is often ill-humored, argumentative, defiant, negative, always "on the defensive," and highly critical of others in an effort to justify his own deep feelings of inadequacy.

The most pathetic and difficult forms of neurotic oppression to deal with are the deep-rooted feelings of *self-pity* and the abnormal *desire for attention* found in some individuals. They have had a dread of being alone for any length of time and have need of constant companionship and conversation. They often feel mistreated, misunderstood, misrepresented, and disliked by others. Frequently, they develop some psychosomatic ailment or disease, as a result of the subconscious desire for attention, in order to find escape through sickness from the problems and perplexities of life. Such persons are called "hypochondriacs" and seek to control and manipulate others by the shrewd use of their illness, their households and families being forced to adjust to their abnormal life and whims, sacrificing everything for their personal comfort. Such neurotics are often overly conscious of their health and welfare, being alarmed at the slightest symptom and usually contact their physician on the slightest pertext. Attention with themselves is their only real interest and they expect others to follow suit. In their affliction they have found an excuse for failing to meet their obligations, or to attain their level for aspiration in business, marriage, religion, or life in general. Their life is characterized as "just one great bundle of problems and anxieties" as they journey from one person to another—doctor, psychologists, psychiatrist, minister, parents, friends or strangers alike—seeking, always seeking attention, reassurance, advice or help.

Those who are oppressed or possessed with these spirits of self-pity, self-centeredness, and self-love (narcissism) are very difficult to bring to a point of liberation due to the nature of the spirit causing this condition. The victims fear that admission of the real nature of their neurotic condition and deliverance from it will cause them to lose the attention and pity they feel they need to survive. These spirits, unlike many other types, have such a firm hold on their victims, and are so closely identified with their personalities, that these individuals willingly accept such an abnormal disposition as their own. Even after liberation, such persons usually require prayer support, and firm, but loving admonishment to practice standing alone, to face their responsibilities on their own, and to discipline themselves to regular periods of Bible study and prayer in order to develop a strong life of faith. A daily, positive confession of what they have and are in Christ is necessary, together with a firm, steadfast resistance to the temptation to fall back into their previous bondage and dependence upon others.

Compulsive thoughts and behavior, as well as certain phobias and obsessions, are often present in such individuals. Compulsive lying, deception, infidelity, arson, or cleptomania (an irresistible desire to steal, without regard to personal needs) are some of the compulsive abnormalities. Others are obsessed with peculiar and strange ideas. One may, for example, be obsessed with the idea that he will contract some disease as cancer or tuberculosis; another believes that he will die permaturely from the same organic trouble that seems "to run in the family," and from which some of his relations have in fact died. Others sometimes become obsessed with the ideas that they have committed the "unpardonable sin," or that they have failed God, or their families, or their employers, thus living a tormented life of self-condemnation. Those who are obsessed as ruled by some idea or thought (which often has no basis in fact) until it becomes the dominating factor in their lives. Obsessions may be in the form of self-torturing jealousy, or the notion that someone is always watching or following behind, the individual's eyes darting furtively here and there constantly, or the housewife who feels all her friends and neighbors are always talking about her. The compulsions may be in the form of phobias, such as a fear of germs, reflected in the neurotic behavior of the woman who felt compelled to disinfect all the doorknobs in her home daily, never touching one anywhere without wearing gloves to avoid contamination. Some persons are obsessed with a spirit of self-importance, suspicion, covetousness, or pride. Other compulsives cannot keep from repeating the same actions over and over, such as recounting the money which they have just counted because they feel they made a mistake the first time, and then this must be repeated again for the same reason, or such repetitive actions as washing one's hands over and over, retracing one's steps, or repeating instructions again and again. Such compulsions and obsessions often indicate the presence and work of demonic spirits who mercilessly vex and delude their victims.

In summary, the most common characteristics of mental and emotional disturbances and abnormalities as a result of occult involvement, which are found again and again, are: mental illness; serious depression; anxieties and fear; thoughts of self-destruction; compulsive thoughts and behavior; obsessions; emotional instability and self-pity; profound feelings of inadequacy and failure, as well as enslavement to certain excessive appetites, passions and habits.

II. *Psychic Disturbances and Abnormalities.*

Under this category are to be found those forms of subjection and oppression that pertain particularly to the extrasensory functions of the mind or psyche (spirit).

1. *Occult Subjection.*

Those who have had occult involvement of any kind, or who may come from a background in which the family history contains occult connections, frequently become "psychic" themselves and discover that they have certain extrasensory abilities, psychic sensitivity, or abnormal intellectual powers and knowledge at times beyond their normal capacity. These so-called psychic "gifts," resulting from occult connections, are under the control and influence of the powers of darkness and are to be repudiated without reservation, inasmuch as they are under the condemnation of God.[1] The following characteristics indicate occult subjection and will ultimately issue in mental, spiritual, and/or physical deterioration and damage, unless one is liberated from such enslavement by Christ. One may, of course, possess these psychic or ESP powers to a greater or lesser degree than defined here. Moreover, it is to be kept in mind that the characteristics which follow, although they will include the psychic powers and practices of such occult professionals or practitioners as fortune-tellers, astrologists, spiritualist mediums and hypnotists, nevertheless, have primary reference to any and all who have had involvement in occultism in any way.

(1) *Clairvoyance.*

This term describes the psychic ability of some subjected individuals to see objects or events spontaneously and super-normally beyond the natural range of vision. It is the awareness or knowledge of what is taking place elsewhere. This so-called gift of "second sight," which is a satanic counterfeit of the Biblical prophetic gift of the "seer," and the gift of the "word of knowledge" (1 Cor. 12), enables the sensitive to see things relating to the past, present, and sometimes the future (precognition). Clairaudience, the ability to hear voices and sounds supernormally not within the reach of the normal senses, may also be present in such individuals. Persons who are clairvoyant many times have premonitions of death or misfortune concerning others before the event occurs; hear spirit voices, or the alleged voice of a departed loved one or friend giving advice, warning, or assurance of some kind; often discern such things as the substance of a letter before opening it, or know who is calling when the phone rings before answering it; and are subject to dreams and visions of a psychic or bizarre nature.

(2) *Precognition.*

The power of precognition enables occultly subjected persons to have knowledge of, or the ability to see, future events before they occur. Some persons who have become "psychic" through occult associations have this ability to sense or foresee an event that is to take place in the future in a very pronounced way. They often mysteriously experience premonitions of impending events as, for example, Jeane Dixon's prediction of President Kennedy's assassination, or Edgar Cayce's prediction of two World Wars and the years they would begin and end, as well as the universal Depression of 1929. Many persons have precognitive experiences, such as premonitions, visions, dreams, or mental "flashes," whereby they, as a result of becoming "sensitive" psychically through their occult involvement, see, hear, or sense events which are yet future.

(3) *Telepathy.*

Persons who are psychic often exhibit the power of the transference of thought from one mind to another, either by thoughtsending or mind-reading. When the term ESP is mentioned, often this is what is first thought of. Some individuals, after participation in some form of occultism, discover that at times they have the distinct impression that they know what another person is thinking, and which at times is confirmed to them. The ability to "tune in" on another's thoughts and read his mind is an established fact well attested to by many parapsychologists, and by such organizations as the *American Society for Psychical Research*. When one dabbles in occultism, or seeks to heighten his so-called ESP powers through the practice of telepathy, he may find mental images and strong feelings, emotions and thoughts from the minds of others floating into his own consciousness. Often he may not be aware of what is taking place and may interpret these impressions as mere coincidence. Moreover, what may seem at first to be an interesting psychic phenomenon, may often become a mental burden to one psychically sensitive in this way as he is constantly subject to the infiltration of disturbing mental images and thoughts both from the powers of darkness and other minds, often experiencing the same problems and distrubances as the one to whom he is telepathically attuned.

Furthermore, it is possible for one to become "psychically dependent" upon another through the practice of telepathy, hypnotism, or remote influence. With regard to the latter, there are those who unwittingly advocate the use of a form of telepathy known as "remote or unconscious influence." This is an attempt to influence the subconscious mind of others while they are asleep or unconscious by implanting, through suggestion, positive thoughts of love by speaking to the subconscious mind of one who has grown cold or indifferent, for example, or implanting corrective ideas into the subconscious mind of one who might be offended or unreceptive if such advice were given to them openly, or it may take the form of healing therapy, and so on. However, the psychic dangers in such attempts to control and influence the thoughts and behavior of others should be obvious, since the same telepathic powers can and have been used for evil purposes. Adepts of ESP well know that through this power they can influence others, often causing them to think or do as they wish. No finite human being has the right, whatever his alleged motive, to invade the privacy of the subconscious mind of another individual without his consent! God alone has this prerogative and there is no Biblical basis whatever for this practice by Christians. Aside from the obvious dangers involved and the unauthorized intrusion into the mind of another without his permission, it would seem that this is an attempt to circumvent the Biblical method of solving one's problems; namely, the prayer of faith. Do such individuals realize that in their attempts to influence the subconscious minds of others by speaking to them while they are asleep that they are intruding upon the prerogatives of God, and may also be establishing telepathic connections with their minds unconsciously which may later have adverse effect? The occult nature of this practice, which is condemned in Scripture as *charming* and *enchantment* (Deut. 18:10-11), and which is little more than "mesmerism" of the subconscious, should be repudiated by the Christian without hesitation as an abomination to God. Moreover, those who presently teach and practice remote influence, advocating its use by other Christians, should seriously consider the insidious nature of this practice and its disharmony with the teachings of Scripture.

(4) *Divination.*

This is the most common form of occultism and has reference to the ancient black art of fortunetelling, whether by the crystal ball, palm reading, cards, pendulum, ouija board, planchette, glass tumbler moving, tea leaves, handwriting analysis (graphology), horoscope, or any of the many other forms of divination. Fortunetelling differs from clairvoyance in that what the clairvoyant sees or knows comes to him spontaneously, whereas the individual who practices any form of fortunetelling divines by use of certain occult objects, such as cards, tea leaves, ouija board, crystal ball, and so forth, or practices soothsaying by interpreting signs, omens, dreams, or other phenomena.

Millions of victims are being drawn into the abominable web of occultism either by visits to fortunetellers or by participation in some form of occult practice, whether consciously, or unconsciously, by playing with such "games" as ouija, ESP, telepathy, using fortune-telling cards, and so on. It must be emphasized that those who have participated in these forms of occult practice, even though it was done "in fun" have, nevertheless, opened themselves to the same occult oppression and subjection as those who are seriously involved. The same dark powers exercise influence and control over all forms of occultism. A loaded revolver is just as dangerous when one is only playing a "game" of Russian roulette as it would be in the hands of one attempting to commit suicide. Some, who through experience have suffered occult oppression or subjection, warn of the dangers of innocently fooling around with the psychic and occult in the form of ESP, telepathy, ouija boards, automatic writing, and table-tipping, for instance. Such persons, whether they know it or not, are inviting invisible (demonic) "playmates" to participate in the game or practice with them and are in for a rude awakening psychically and spiritually, often of a permanent nature.

(5) *Psychometry.*

This is the psychic ability to determine the facts about an object's owner from contact with the object. For example, simply by touching the picture or some personal object belonging to a missing person, such a "sensitive" individual can give the particulars of the person, their present whereabouts, and whether or not the individual is living or dead. Other psychometrics are able to diagnose diseases and other ailments merely by handling an object belonging to the afflicted person, by touching the patient's body, or by use of the pendulum. Our files contain testimonies of those who suffered oppression as a result of contact with such psychic healers, from which deliverance from the powers of darkness was necessary.

(6) *Radiesthesia.*

Divining for such things as water, oil, and minerals, using a dowsing rod or pendulum, is an ancient occult practice known the world over, having its roots in heathenism, and is condemned in the Scriptures (Hosea 4:12; Deut. 18:10) as inspired and controlled by "the spirit of fornication" (an unclean spirit). Martin Luther charged, and rightly so, that the practice violated the First Commandment. A recent geological survey on water dowsing, often called "water witching," stated there were an estimated 25,000 water dowsers in the United States alone. The actual number of nonprofessional dowsers is much higher. It is practiced by water engineers in many localities to locate water pipes, by plumbers to determine sewer lines, by well drillers to find water sources, by mining engineers to locate minerals or oil, and by the Marine Corps in Vietnam to locate hidden mines, tunnels, and booby-traps along jungle trails. Practical training in the use of the dowsing rod is a part of the official training program at Camp Pendleton, California. Thousands of officers and men have been subjected to these dark powers (although done voluntarily in each case) and only time will tell the terrible psychic effect upon these men as a result of their occult involvement.

The common form of dowsing for water is by use of a forked stick, such as a hazel or willow twig. Other objects are also employed such as coat-hangers, wires, keys on a chain hanging from a Bible, and brass welding rods. Some persons with this occult ability are able to use the pendulum successfully also (such things are used in the manner of a pendulum as a small ball or pear shaped object hanging from a string or chain; a needle, key, or ring on a string or thread, etc.). The pendulum (or dowsing rod) is used to divine for gold, silver, oil, water, minerals, buried treasure, missing persons, and many other things by holding the pendulum (or rod) over a map of the area in question until the divining instrument reacts in a certain manner at the correct location.[2] Of course, the divining instruments are also used at the geographical sites themselves in the general area where water, minerals, missing objects or persons, and oil are believed to be. Radiesthesia, or use of the dowsing rod or pendulum, is frequently used in the diagnosis of illness and disease, to determine the sex of an unborn baby, to prescribe medicines, in aiding in crime detection, and in any of the ways in which psychometry (5) may be utilized. Those who practice dowsing or use the pendulum frequently give evidence of psychic disturbances and other signs of occult subjection or oppression.

(7) *Magic Practices.*

Occult activity on the part of one subjected by occultism is often seen in the form of involvement in such magical practices as hypnosis, mental suggestion, remote influence of others, magic charming, conjuring and healing animals and humans, casting spells, concocting and using magical remedies and cures, and countless other magical and superstitious practices. Magical influence and practices often play an important role in the lives of those subjected to occultism. It should be pointed out that the source is the same (satanic) whether one practices so-called "white" magic (invoking the hidden powers for good ends), or "black" magic (invoking the spirits for destructive or evil purposes).

Incredible as it may seem, nevertheless, even in this modern scientific age millions are now, or have been at some time, involved in some manner with ancient magic practices and rites, ranging from the charming of warts and burns to the use of spells, magic herbs, and hex signs on houses and barns (which can still be seen in some areas). Magic practices and beliefs are not limited to rural folk, who are often naturally superstitious, but are to be found in the urban areas and large cities. That these practices are not mere, harmless superstitions can be seen time and again in the adverse psychic, mental, spiritual, and physical effects in the lives of countless people involved. Simply stated, magic is man's sinful attempt to break through the bounds set by God and His Providence, as well as other persons, for one's own selfish purposes.

One of the most subtle and potentially dangerous forms of magical practice is hypnosis, an ancient occult method of influence or control of the mind and actions of others. Largely through the efforts of the Viennese physician, Mesmer, and through its adoption by psychiatrists, dentists, doctors, and psychologists, hypnotism has lost much of its distasteful association with witchcraft and the vaudeville stage, and has now acquired a cloak of respectability. The ancient "charmer" and "enchanter" (Deut. 18:10-11) now, as often as not, has a Ph.D. degree!

Advocates often try to justify this ancient form of witchcraft by arguing that hypnotherapy has many beneficial uses medically, and that no hypnotist can compel his subject to commit any criminal action or morally wrong act which the subjected individual would not do when awake. Both these premises are erroneous. In the first place, hypnotism seldom has any permanent effects when used, for instance, in the treatment of many psychological, mental, moral, and emotional problems. One may, for example, be told while under hypnosis that he has been released from his deep-seated fears, doubts, or the problem of alcoholism, but the effect of such suggestions will seldom be lasting and will have to be repeated in time. This is due to the fact that the *cause* of such conditions has not been removed, the *effect* only being treated. Moreover, any attempt to relieve symptoms through hypnosis can be particularly dangerous, as many professional hypnotists and hypnotherapists attest, when treatment focuses merely on the symptoms and does not deal with the underlying causes. One doctor cites the case in which a patient, through hypnosis, was stopped from chain smoking, but became a compulsive eater as a result. Cured of her overeating, she became an alcoholic! Such examples are by no means the exception and weaken the naive idea currently held by many that hypnotherapy is a magic "cure-all" in the hands of the medical technician and psychiatrist which can solve all our mental, emotional, social, and psychological problems. The hypnotherapist may remove the symptom without curing the cause and thereby weaken the subject's defenses against inner turmoils and problems. In a neurotic person, for example, the symptom may be only the outward indication of serious inner disturbances. An alcoholic may not be suffering merely from a bad habit, but from a serious neurosis. A physical affliction such as stuttering may be relieved through hypnosis, but be replaced by neurotic tensions which affect the entire personality, or relief from migraine headaches through hypnotherapy may be replaced by some form of psychosis.

In the second place, contrary to popular opinion, many times cases of crime and immoral acts have been performed by those under subjection to someone else through hypnosis, who would not have done so in their conscious state of mind. When one surrenders his will to another individual, he then wills to do what the person who hypnotized him wishes, even performing ridiculous or morally reprehensible acts, if the hypnotist uses the correct techniques of suggestion. For example, a hypnotized individual may be led to disrobe in public if told that he is in the privacy of his own bedroom. Recently, the newspapers reported the case of a woman under hypnosis by her paramour, who engaged in a plot to murder her husband. Women have been abused, crimes committed, and other scandalous acts performed while under hypnosis.

In addition, many young people, encouraged by the cheap literature on the newsstands popularizing the subject, are practicing hypnotism on one another, sometimes with serious consequences in the area of mental, emotional, and psychic damage. Not only is there the danger in amateur hypnotism of inducing psychoneuroses or arousing deep-seated complexes, compulsions, phobias, and other mental and emotional distrubances of long standing, with which the stage hypnotist and novice lacking proper knowledge of the functioning of the mind and emotions cannot cope, but when one surrenders his will to another in this way he is susceptible to hypnotic suggestion from then on. Moreover, he sometimes becomes "psychically dependent" upon the other person, a danger also encountered in telepathy, especially when these practices are repeated.

However, the greatest threat lies in the fact that in the hypnotized state of the surrendered will, the individual is open to the invasion of evil spirits, inasmuch as he must, in order to be hypnotized, relinquish the one divinely endowed moral and spiritual safeguard against such intrusion—the personal will and the power to exercise it freely and independently; or to state it concisely, he has at this time forfeited his independent, moral right to say "yes" or "no." So-called medical and therapeutic hypnosis obviously has no safeguards against this danger any more than the amateur hypnotist has. Demons have admitted through the lips of those possessed by them that the power behind the hypnotist is Satan himself! The moral and spiritual implications involved in hypnotism of any sort should be obvious to any thinking person.

(8) *Spiritism and Mediumistic Powers.*

In addition to the extrasensory powers of clairvoyance, telepathy, divination, psychometry, and so forth, certain other paranormal or psychic abilities which can result from occult subjection are as follows: the ability of self-induced trance states; contact with spirit writing; levitation (the lifting or floating of objects); astral projection (projection of the spirit or psyche out of the body to another place); table-tipping; spirit knockings or rappings; telekinesis (objects are caused to move mysteriously about the room; musical instruments play as by unseen hands);

apports (articles made to appear in locked rooms); materializations (the power to materialize the alleged spirit of the dead into visible form, as well as other things); parakinesis (PK, or the ability to control objects by the power of the mind and will), and many other forms of psychic phenomena. These occult and psychic powers are found not only in those who are practicing mediums, but also some of these phenomena and paranormal abilities may be found frequently in those who have had occult associations.

Involvement in occultism often results, as we have seen, in subjection to these powers to such a degree that the individual is almost, if not totally, dependent upon fortunetellers for information and advice, astrologers for guidance in the daily affairs of business and life, magical practices for healing, controlling the forces of nature, or influencing others, and so on, until the victim is hopelessly entangled in a labyrinth of evil influences and control.

2. *Occult Oppression.*

The foregoing forms of psychic powers and extrasensory abilities, which result from occult involvement, are indicative of occult "subjection," that is, such persons have been brought into subjection to the powers of darkness (although they do not always recognize their source), and as a result of having opened themselves to these demonic forces they have become "psychically" subjected. However, occult participation does not always result in such sensitivity, there often being only some form of "oppression" occurring. In any event, oppression in some form will be the final outcome, with those who have become "psychic" or clairvoyant usually suffering the most severely. At this point we shall note the most significant forms of psychic *oppression* which result from occult involvement.

(1) *Poltergeist Phenomena.*

Poltergeist (German for "noisy ghost") manifestations are not uncommon phenomena, being observed by many reliable witnesses, and may be atributed to the malicious works perpetrated by demonic spirits in order to harass their victims who are suffering the consequences of their occult involvement.

In this instance, the oppressed individual suffers definite psychic attacks in the form of such bizarre occurrences as follows: objects are seen floating about the room, sometimes falling with a loud crash to the floor as though thrown by some unseen power; mysterious fires break out about the residence; strange noises, rappings, and knockings are heard; often there is heard the sound of the rattling of chains, moaning, weeping or crying; disembodied spirit voices speak threats and obscenities; articles suddenly appear or disappear in closed and locked rooms; furniture moves about the room when no one is near it; the piano begins to play in the middle of the night by unseen hands, which may be followed by the bed suddenly rising off the floor and the covers unceremoniously yanked from over its victim; doors mysteriously open and are slammed shut; the doorbell begins to ring incessantly, the frightful confusion ceasing upon investigation as suddenly as it began; light bulbs burst; rocks, dirt, broken glass and other rubble pour down through the ceiling leaving no trace of how they entered, for the ceiling remains undisturbed; all the lights in the house suddenly flash on and off; phantom footsteps are heard on the stairs, or strange noises, such as a trunk sliding across the floor, are heard coming from the attic, together with other puzzling phenomena. Stones and china are sometimes thrown about with abandon, furniture is upset, personal objects are hidden from the owner or disappear, and it is not uncommon for violent and vicious attacks to be made upon the victim himself.

Incredible as it may seem, nevertheless, few people seem to have noted the relationship between this form of oppression and occult involvement on the part of the victim, and as a result even Christians have been unable to cope properly with it in their attempts at liberation of the oppressed. Unless one deals with such oppression from an occult standpoint, then there can be no assurance of deliverance and liberation from this form of psychic or poltergeist attacks. Although it is recognized that poltergeist activities sometimes are confined to the particular residence or area in which they occur, and are often the result of seances, Spiritualist meetings, or some other form of occult activities being conducted there at some time; nevertheless, the individual suffering such oppression is usually undergoing these attacks in consequence of some past or present occult connections on his part, or in his family history. From our own counselling experiences further evidence for this is seen in the fact that before liberation one individual had continued to suffer such oppression even after moving to other places of residence.

(2) *Apparitions, Specters, Monstrous Phantasms.*

Appearances of ghostly figures, specters, and demonic creatures (often mistaken for mere hallucinations) such as headless figures, weird animals, or other hideous creatures are frequently found in the experiences of those who have had occult connections of some kind. One oppressed victim was almost driven insane when, upon smelling fire and brimstone in the room, turned and saw, what appeared to be, a filthy, slimy demonic creature in the room; another was confronted by a headless body, and another by a faceless specter upon opening the door. Such things as dwarfs; dark, ugly, leering faces; disembodied hands; serpents, and other fearsome phantasms are sometimes seen. Often, as a portent warning of an accident to occur to a friend or relative, or warning of their death or serious illness, the voice or apparition of this person will be manifested to the oppressed individual at the moment of the tragedy or shortly thereafter. Others suffering occult oppression sense the presence at times of an invisible intelligence or some oppressive, dark creature or power, which may seem to lurk about the room, or even follow its victim about. At times there is experienced an actual attack by these malevolent spirits, the victim being choked, bitten, throttled, or molested in some other way. Psychic attacks in the form of persistent nightmares are also common.

(3) *Incubi and Succubae Experiences.*

This is an attempted assault upon a human by an unclean spirit or demon of lust for the purpose of gratifying its sexual appetites. Both women and men are known to have suffered such attempts at sexual molestation, as well as actual attacks. The reality of such experiences is confirmed both from history and the writer's counselling experience. By taking Genesis 6:1-4; 2 Peter 2:4 and Jude 6-7 in their literal sense, there also seems to be adequate Scriptural basis for the reality of such bizarre occurrences.

III. *Spiritual Subjection and Oppression.*

From the religious standpoint occult involvement invariably affects one spiritually, frequently causing serious damage to one's spiritual life and faith. The spiritual effects and influence of the powers of darkness are readily apparent in the symptoms which follow, not all of which would necessarily be found in any one individual, nor to the same degree. Often there is progressive spiritual deterioration and disintegration in the area of faith unless deliverance is effected, inasmuch as these dark influences continue their destructive work, although the individual is (or later becomes) a Christian, and even though occult participation may have been relatively nominal, or took place several years previously.

1. *Indifference to Spiritual Things.*

Spiritual deterioration is seen in a noticeable indifference to the Word of God, prayer, worship, and spiritual matters in general, often against one's will, with little success at overcoming this state, although repeated attempts to prevail over increasing spiritual apathy are made.

2. *Serious Problems Concerning Doubt and Unbelief.*

Extreme and persistent doubts concerning the teachings of Scripture, especially the supernatural, or difficulty in exercising faith, are clear evidence of spiritual deterioration as a result of occult associations. Many times these individuals are seemingly powerless against the temptation to doubt, waver, question, and distrust God, His promises, and His ministers, at times feeling almost overwhelmed by skepticism, suspicion, incredulity, disbelief, indecision, and other misgivings.

3. *Religious Aberrations.*

Religious delusions, heresies, and errors, ranging from agnosticism to affirming the doctrines of Spiritualism, Modernism, or the false religious cults, are symptomatic of occult subjection. Such abnormalities are pious self-righteousness; spiritual pride; hypocrisy; religious extremes, such as abnormal aversion to certain foods, serious deviations from Scripture in doctrine or practice, asceticism, and extreme antagonism toward other religious bodies or Christian groups, are also found.

4. *Inability to Receive the Holy Spirit.*

Frequently, there is found to be a spiritual barrier in those with occult associations when they wish to receive the baptism in the Holy Spirit, although the experience sometimes is earnestly desired and sought for years. Liberation from occult powers, which act as hindrances, is the only solution we have found.

5. *Resistance.*

A very significant indication of the spiritual effect upon those who have had occult involvement is the resistance sometimes evidenced by some to the teaching concerning the reality of occult subjection and oppression, as well as indifference to the dangers involved. One of the characteristic marks of occult delusion and enslavement is this opposition and resistance found in some of those who have been guilty of occult sins. This hostile reaction is often the result of a spirit of pride which prevents them from admitting their gullibility, sin and delusion. This resistance is sometimes motivated by their reluctance to sever their occult connections. Moreover, the powers of darkness struggle against being discovered and removed from their position of influence and control. However, the very act of resistance itself, in view of the plain teachings of Scripture condemning these practices, is evidence enough of occult subjection in such individuals.

Such resistance is often expressed in the form of unwillingness on the part of the oppressed individual to accept the fact that a Christian can be oppressed by Satan, even though this individual usually is suffering such oppression at the time! He, of course, charges his problems, for which he is seeking help, to some other source or to causes unknown. Experience has shown that the source of such resistance to the fact of occult oppression and subjection must be recognized and admitted, and the powers of darkness resisted in faith at this point by the oppressed or subjected person, or deliverance from their condition is impossible.

6. *Occult Bondage and Opposition to God.*

In many instances where spiritual damage is severe, the person is in such a state of bondage to the powers of darkness that there are evidenced the following forms of occult subjection: inability of the individual to believe on or confess Christ, in spite of the fact that such individuals frequently would like to believe; the inability to pray or read the Word of God (often there is experienced extreme drowsiness, or the inability to concentrate at such times); inability to keep one's attention on the preaching or teaching of the Scriptures, as well as difficulty in understanding them; the inability to acknowledge the fact of the efficacy of the blood Atonement, or the Deity of Christ; and the infiltration of unclean thoughts and sexual images into the mind when any attempt at spiritual devotions or exercises is made. There will often be found a dependence upon the enslavement to various forms of occultism also.

Opposition to God, as seen in the following characteristics, is unmistakable evidence of demon *possession:* blasphemous thoughts against God, Christ, and the Trinity; opposition to the work of the Holy Spirit; aversion to all references to the blood of Christ or His Deity; scorn, mockery, and ridicule toward the Bible, preaching, believers, Christianity, or divine and holy things in general. Also there is often to be found in such persons violent raging, cursing, and blasphemous opposition against all attempts at deliverance, even when such liberation is being sought by the subjected individual himself. Usually, however, there is such bondage to occultism that there is a lack of will power or desire for deliverance from such enslavement.

IV. *Physical Oppression.*

Certain physical symptoms are indicative of the presence and activity of demonic powers. These are related to outward behavior, bodily appearance, and to the physical condition. In some cases, of course, the mere presence of just one of these conditions would not necessarily be symptomatic of demonic oppression and activity, but could be the result of other causes.

1. *Speech and Behavioral Abnormalities.*

The oppressed individual will frequently manifest one or more of the following symptoms, and usually in a noticeably abnormal manner: abnormal talkativeness; unusual loudness of tone and voice; hysterical laughter; persistent restlessness and uneasiness; silliness; giddiness; unusually foolish talk and behavior; incongruity of actions; muttering to oneself; incoherence in speech and thought; compulsive shouting or screaming when provoked; the absence of certain normal reflexes, or the exaggeration of others; peculiar postures (e.g., abornally rigid and ramrod straight; unrelaxed; or the exact opposite state of lethargic, sluggish droopiness); deep sighing, denoting despondency or feelings of self-pity; shunning or withdrawal from public scrutiny; odd, queer eccentricities of speech which are annoyingly repetitious.

In instances of actual demonic possession, especially when the evil spirits within such an individual feel threatened by exposure or expulsion, or when they find themselves in an environment where the power of the blood and the Name of Christ are present, there are frequently to be seen more violent physical manifestations such as: foaming at the mouth; retching; screaming; cursing, blasphemy; raging against Christianity; physical resistance or attempted and threatened violence; and at times, convulsions, with pains and carmps, or a state of catalepsy. At such times the spirits frequently speak through the possessed victim. There will be seen the display of an alien intelligence through the individual foreign to that normally in evidence. At times the possessed individual is able to understand or speak a foreign language which is unknown to him (not to be confused with Biblical tongues, for in the case of possession the demon, who knows the language, is speaking through the person). Frequently, there is knowledge of hidden facts and prognostications of future events given, as well as the display of feats of supernormal strength or supernatural phenomena.

2. *Abnormal Facial Characteristics.*

The face is often seen to be noticeably contorted by fear, chronic doubts, incredulity, or anxiety; or the countenance is strained, uneasy, or tormented. Such individuals seldom smile and there is no joy in their conversation or life. A morbid expression is common and thoughts of suicide are often present. In others, the appearance may be defiant, wicked, scowling, perverse, dark or sullen. At times the complexion is also affected, being dark and somber, or pallid and corpse-like. Other extremes of facial characteristics are seen from a stereotyped, frozen smile or grimace to an expressionless, impassive or stoical indifference.

The eyes are abnormally bright and protruding, or glazed and with a trance-like, or hunted, animal-like stare. In others there is a wicked, defiant glare, or a demonic leering in the eyes.

3. *Abnormal Physical Ailments.*

Chronic, persistent physical ailments, diseases, or pains that do not respond to prayer or treatment of any kind, but which seem to linger on and on, may indicate occult oppression. Where there has been occult involvement, deliverance often depends upon liberation from occult oppression, mere prayer for healing being insufficient, inasmuch as one must deal, in such instances, with the cause of the affliction, not just the effect.

V. *Material, Domestic, and Social Forms of Oppression.*

Most people are unaware of the far-reaching

effects of occult participation. Occult associations can also result in oppression which affects the lives of others, resulting, for example, in serious martial problems, often culminating in divorce (one person traced the beginning of marital strife and incompatibility to the day following a visit to a seance); discord between parents and children; disputes with neighbors; friction and strife between business associates or others, as well as church divisions and irreconcilable schisms.

This form of oppression is the result of divisive and factious spirits whose primary objective is to work in the affairs of men in order to divide, disrupt, confuse, deceive, distract, disturb, perplex and disorganize, seeking thereby in every way to destroy unity, harmony, and peace. Their sole aim is to cause as much affliction, sorrow, agony, anguish, grief, misery, misfortune, privation, distrust, suspicion, doubt, anxiety, and confusion as possible in the daily circumstances of life. Persistent financial distress, material loss, and subjection to poverty, need, scarcity, and other material privations, can also result from occult involvement.

Deliverance from all forms of oppression and subjection resulting from occult involvement can come only in one way, and it is to this that we now turn.

4

LIBERATION FROM OCCULT OPPRESSION AND SUBJECTION

It will first be necessary to deal with two significant questions which sometimes stand as a hindrance in the minds of some individuals who are unaware of the reality and extent of satanic influence and enslavement even among Christians. As a result of erroneous teaching and beliefs, which are based neither upon Scripture nor experience, Satan has deluded many concerning the following questions: Can a Christian be oppressed by Satan, or possess evil spirits? Can one who has never actively participated in any form of occultism by occultly subjected or oppressed? The answer to both these questions is "yes," which fact can be supported both from Scripture and experience.

Believers can be oppressed, vexed, depressed, hindered, bound, and afflicted by Satan, or even suffer infestation by demonic spirits. We are to make a distinction, however, between absolute demon *possession,* in which the life and will is under the dominion and control of Satan, and the *invasion* of the mind or body by malevolent spirits, such as, for example, spirits of infirmity, fear, resentment, doubt, depression, and so on. It is to the latter condition that we have reference when we speak of a Christian suffering "infestation" by evil spirits, not to demon possession per se, as may be seen, for instance, in the account of the Gadarene demoniac in Mark 5:1f. However, inasmuch as malignant spirits can invade the mind or body of a Christian and must be "cast out" before deliverance from the problems which they cause is realized, we must say then that such individuals are oppressed by Satan or infested with evil spirits to which they have yielded for one reason or another.

One may sit in an "ivory tower" and debate the theological possibility of this fact at length, but just one or two encounters with the reality of the powers of darkness in the lives of Christians today can do much in the way of correcting one's theology on this matter we have found. We know from experience that believers can be oppressed and suffer invasion of the mind and body by malicious spirits for the precise reason that the vast majority of those with whom we have dealt and seen God deliver from all forms of demonic oppression and enslavement, resulting from occult involvement, were Christians! Moreover, many of these were believers who had received the baptism in the Holy Spirit. By occult participation, one can open the door to oppression or invasion by the powers of darkness either before or after becoming a Christian.

The fact that believers can be oppressed or suffer infestation by demonic spirits is seen in several instances in the Scriptures. The oppressing misfortunes and physical affliction of Job are said to be the work of Satan (Job 1-2). Even in the House of God there can be those possessed with unclean spirits as Mark 1:23f. clearly teaches: "And there was *in their synagogue* a man with an unclean spirit," whom Jesus set free. There is no reason to doubt that he was a believer who had gone there to worship. The woman bowed together by Satan and delivered of a "spirit of infirmity" by Jesus was also in the synagogue. She was a believer ("a daughter of Abraham") and was said to have been bound by Satan with a spirit of infirmity which was cast out of her (Lk. 13:11-16). Believers may also be implied in 2 Timothy 2:23-26, who need to recover themselves from "the snare of the devil, who are taken captive by him at his will." A believer in the Church at Corinth was doubtless possessed of a spirit of lust, later suffering oppression at the hands of Satan, for the Apostle admonishes the Church to deliver this member "unto Satan for the destruction of the flesh, that the spirit may be saved in the day of the Lord Jesus" (I Cor. 5:1-5). Jesus "rebuked" the fever in Peter's mother-in-law and she was healed (Lk. 4:38-39). Quite obviously, one does not rebuke a mere rise in temperature, but He addressed Himself to a personality, a spirit causing the fever. Jesus uses this same term to rebuke Satan in Mark 8:33, and demons in Mark 9:25. Since the Scriptures teach that all sickness is the "oppression" of Satan (Acts 10:38), it follows then that a Christian who becomes sick or diseased is suffering satanic oppression.

If the oppressed are to be set free, we must rid ourselves of the naive and unscriptural notion that believers cannot be oppressed by Satan, or possess evil spirits in some instances, contending that being a Christian automatically safeguards one against any such invasion. Satan has deluded Christians into believing that since Jesus defeated him at the Cross, we need only to ignore him today; or even if one was oppressed or possessed with spirits before conversion, he is somehow mysteriously set free when saved. If this was true, then why do not blind, deaf, dumb, or epileptic spirits leave upon the conversion of the afflicted person? Why do not cancers and other diseases leave in those oppressed by Satan with these ailments when they are converted to Christ? How is it possible for Christians still to be subject to fear, depression, insanity, disease, and pain if believers cannot be oppressed by the powers of darkness? How, then, do we account for Peter speaking at one moment by divine revelation and the next being moved by Satan to speak words that were soundly rebuked by Christ who addressed His rebuke to Satan himself (Matt. 16:13-23)? Simon, the magician, is said to have believed and been baptized, and there is certainly no reason to exclude him from the number of Samaritans who also received the baptism in the Holy Spirit, yet he had not completely been delivered from his occult bondage and was commanded to repent and pray (Acts 8). If Satan cannot invade the life of a believer, how then was he able to "fill" the hearts of Ananias and Sapphira, two disciples in the early Church (Acts 5:1f.)? One of the strongest arguments against the unscriptural contention that Satan presents no serious threat to the believer is given by the Apostle Paul in 2 Corinthians 12 in which he states that he himself suffered oppression at the hands of "the messenger of Satan" who was allowed to buffet him.

There are two dangerous and unscriptural attitudes toward Satan and his demonic forces. One is to deny, as the liberal theologians do, the reality and existence of a personal adversary, the Devil. On the other hand, it is equally as absurd to do as most contemporary Christians do and treat the subject with an attitude of indifference, being blind to his extensive power and work and deluded by the naive idea that Satan presents no real threat to the believer beyond tempting one to sin now and then. Such an attitude has no basis in Scripture whatever. On the contrary, the Scriptures repeatedly warn believers that they should "be sober, be vigilant; because your adversary the devil, as a roaring lion, walketh about, seeking whom he may *devour:* Whom resist stedfast in the faith" (1 Pet. 5:8-9), and "neither give place to the devil" (Eph. 4:27). The New Testament describes the Christian life as a spiritual warfare, admonishing the believer to "resist the devil" (Jam. 4:7), and to "put on the whole armour of God, that ye may be able to stand against the wiles of the devil. For we wrestle not against flesh and blood, but against principalities, against powers, against the rulers of the darkness of this world, against spiritual wickedness in high places" (Eph. 6:11-12). Scripture abounds in references to a spiritual conflict, which the believer is to take seriously, against an evil, cunning, powerful Adversary who rules over a vast, highly organized kingdom, consisting of principalities, powers, and world rulers of the darkness of this age. He is designated as "the prince of the power of the air," "the ruler of this world," and "the god of this age." When he offered Jesus the kingdoms of this world in return for His worship of him, the Lord did not challenge his right to offer them, for the precise reason that they belong to him. His chief strategy, therefore, is to convince believers that he does not have to be taken seriously, and, as a result, he has been able to achieve tremendous victories over men in many instances. To see the folly in the unscriptural notion that Satan presents no serious threat to the believer, one needs only to recall some of the instances given in Scripture of his victories in the lives of the unwary and careless such as, for example, the fall of Adam and Eve from their state of sinlessness, together with all their posterity; the yielding of King Saul to an evil spirit and his tragic end; the sin of David and its consequences; the apostasy of Judas, one of the twelve Apostles; the denial of Christ by Peter, who was also an Apostle; the influence of Satan in the lives of Ananias and Sapphira, two of the first disciples in the early Church; the incestuous sin in the life of a member in the Corinthian Church; the desertion of Paul by Demas, a fellow-worker of the Apostle, who returned to the world, giving up Christianity; the excommunication of Hymeneus and Alexander in consequence of their loss of the true faith; as well as the sins and low moral and spiritual state of several of the first-century Christian Churches mentioned in the Book of Revelation, which necessitated the sharp rebuke by Christ. To this may be added the prophetic warnings of Scripture concerning the great end-time apostasy and falling away as a result of satanic and demonic influence and work; e.g., 2 Thessalonians 2:1f; 1 Timothy 4:1f.; 2 Timothy 3:1f; Matthew 24:24; Revelation 13:1f; Acts 20:28-31.

Thus, the Scriptures plainly forewarn believers that there will be some who will be influenced by Satan, being drawn away by his deceptions, for "the Spirit speaketh expressly, that in the latter times some shall depart from the faith, giving heed to seducing spirits, and doctrines of devils" (1 Tim. 4:1). It should be carefully noted that it is said here that some shall *"depart from the faith."* Quite clearly, it is only an individual who professes faith that can "depart" from the faith, as unbelievers were never in the faith. Of the disciples Hymeneus and Alexander it is said that they "thrust away" the faith from them. Moreover, the Scriptures show that Satan has at times been able to discourage believers through trials, tempting them to turn away from Christ (Heb. 3; 6; 10); hinder believers (1 Thess. 2:18), or even an angel (Dan. 10:12-13); deceive believers (1 Tim. 1:18-20; 2:14); speak through believers (Matt. 16:21-23); influence believers (Jam. 3:14-15; Acts 5:1f.); destroy their possessions (Job 1); afflict them with disease (Job 2), destroy their flesh (1 Cor. 5), or bind them with a spirit of infirmity (Lk. 13:11f.); oppress them (2 Cor. 12:7); and sift them as wheat (Lk. 22:31-32). Satanic oppression is to be found in the lives of many saints. In addition to the Apostle Paul, who was oppressed by "the angel or messenger of Satan," demons and the Devil were very real to Anthony of Egypt, who had many a conflict with them face to face, and Tertullian speaks of the opposition of demons to Christians whom they seek to terrify and injure. Luther tells of repeated attempts by Satan to interfere with him and his ministry by direct attacks from the Enemy in the form of ghostly noises, poltergeist phenomena, and other weird occurrences, the Devil once even manifesting himself to him. The Wesley family also underwent poltergeist attacks, which disturbed the peace of the rectory at nights with loud knocks, raps on the walls and beds, phantom footsteps, objects flying about mysteriously and apparitions. St. Teresa suffered much vexation and oppression at the hands of Satan, experiencing at times direct attacks spiritually, mentally, and physically, as did the Cure d'Ars, Jean-

Marie Vianney, A.B. Simpson, and many others. In setting forth the Scriptural basis for the reality of satanic oppression and demonic attacks upon the believer, we are not, of course, overlooking the fact of the believer's victory in Christ over Satan and the powers of darkness, as well as his place of authority with Christ in the heavenlies, far above all principalities and powers (Eph. 2:6; Col. 2:12-15), but we are wisely recognizing, as the contemporary Church has failed to do, that the first rule in effective warfare is to know your enemy, his methods, strength, and tactics.

There are some Christians who feel compelled to admit (in view of the evidence) that it is possible for a Christian to be oppressed, depressed, attacked and vexed by evil spirits, yet they cannot accept the fact that a Christian can be infested with such spirits. It seems, however, merely a matter of semantics to split "theological hairs" over terminology as to whether or not a Christian is being "oppressed" by Satan when he is suffering from a cancer or mental illness at his hands, or whether an evil spirit has actually "invaded" his body or mind, inasmuch as the source and result are the same! In either event it is with Satan that we must deal if liberation is to come. In recognizing this fact, we are not, however, overlooking the need for distinguishing between oppression and possession by malevolent spirits, there being the need for exorcising these spirits in the latter case, whereas prayer is usually sufficient in the case of oppression.

To the fact that Christians not only can be

oppressed by demons, but also infested with them, many reliable witnesses agree. Dr. V. R. Edman, former President of Wheaton College, said in reply to the question of the possibility of a Christian possessing demonic spirits that theory would say, "no," but the facts say, "yes." Theoretically a demon cannot possess a body in which the Holy Spirit resides, but Dr. Edman said that he knew of true Christians who were truly demon possessed and who were delivered by prayer in Jesus' Name. In my personal experience, the majority of those for whom I have prayed for deliverance from occult oppression or subjection were Christians, including ministers and the wives of ministers.

Gordon Lindsay writes: "It is a matter of grave concern, to observe the number of ways that demons are attacking, harrassing, and actually dominating people who are professing Christians." Dr. Russell Meade, on the basis of his experience in the deliverance of Christians, points out in his book on demonism today, that there is no Biblical evidence for thinking that the Holy Spirit and a demon cannot inhabit the same body. H.A. Maxwell Whyte writes, "... we have seen hundreds of people manifestly delivered from all kinds of evil spirits... We have found that our young people have needed this strong prayer of deliverance... Many today are being set free from unclean spirits... Remember these young people for whom we have prayed are members of Christian Churches." He continues, "Most Christians are far more bound by Satan and his legions than they realize, or will readily admit. The whole subject is shrouded in mystery and fear. Pride will not permit us to admit a need, and to permit another to pray for us." "The objection is frequently made," writes A.J. MacMillan, "that a true child of God cannot be brought thus under the power of the enemy. Experience disproves this, for even spiritual believers and earnest and successful workers have suffered...." Dr. Kurt E. Koch in his book on occultism cites numerous instances in his ministry of Christians needing liberation from occult subjection and oppression. A well known evangelist in America, after relating the experiences of a missionary who became possessed by tormenting, malevolent spirits, suffering terribly until deliverance, states that he believes that similar experiences may be more common among Christians than we suppose.

The question has been asked by some individuals who have had occult involvement before their conversion to Christ, although none since, "How is it possible for a Christian still to be suffering oppression or subjection because of this earlier preconversion participation?" The answer to this is not difficult; it is because the "door," which they opened to the powers of darkness by such occult participation, will remain open to these oppressing spirits until such individuals, by a definite act of faith and personal exercise of the will, close the door against such satanic invasion. If I were to open the door of my home to a murderer, thief, and reprobate and invite him in before my conversion, the criminal would not automatically vacate the premises merely because I have now changed my interests, but he must be ejected from the house and the door closed and locked against further intrusion. All occult participation, regardless of the kind or degree of involvement, is an open invitation for the powers of darkness to invade the premises, and Satan does not withdraw his influences and work until commanded to do so, for he claims certain "trespass rights" in the life of such individuals. We are not dealing with mere theological theory as to the doctrinal "possibility" of such invasions by the powers of darkness in the lives of believers, but with the reality of the fact of such oppression and subjection based upon the teachings of Scripture and upon experience. There is an abundance of evidence for those who care to investigate the matter to prove that just because one turns his back upon occult participation after becoming a Christian does not mean that the powers of darkness have turned their back upon him!

A second significant question which must be clarified before discussing the way of liberation from occult oppression and subjection is, "Can a Christian who has never actively participated in any form of occultism be occultly subjected or oppressed?"

We have found many times that a person who has never actively participated in any form of occult practice can, nevertheless, suffer oppression or subjection, experiencing what may be termed "passive" oppression or subjection by these powers. Just as disease can be inherited by the innocent from one's ancestors, and just as moral degeneracy and undesirable traits, such as uncontrollable anger, dissipation, or intemperance, for example, may be found in the offspring of such parents, so too children, whose parents and/or blood relations have had occult contacts, ofren suffer various forms of occult bondage and oppression. Christians, who in childhood were subjected to occult influences, often find that they too need liberation from the powers of darkness, which have gained access and are oppressing them in mind, body, or in some other manner.

It is not our purpose to attempt to convince the skeptics of the reality of passive oppression, but to help those who, although they know of no active participation in occult practices on their part, are, nevertheless, suffering some form of oppression for reasons unknown to themselves. In our files are records of individuals suffering forms of "passive" oppression or subjection of every description, such as, for example, chronic fear or doubt, uncontrollable lust, persistent illness, emotional instability, or depression. Others tell of suffering incubi assaults; of hearing spirit voices; of seeing demonic apparitions; of possessing clairvoyant and psychic powers, and so on, all of which result, not from their active occult participation, but either from the occult involvements of their relatives, or from having been innocently subjected to occult influences as children. For instance, passive subjection and oppression have occurred as a result of the victim being taken to an occult "healer" as a child to have warts removed, burns healed, or diseases cured by magic charming or other occult means. Others were made subject to oppression as a result of being taken to Spiritualist meetings, or other false religious cults (Theosophy, Rosicrucian, Christian Science, Unity, etc.) as children. Again, passive oppression or subjection has been found in children whose parents or grandparents have been involved in seances, fortunetelling, or other forms of spiritism and occultism. The Scriptures give evidence of the innocent suffering oppression by Satan and sometimes possession by evil spirits, as, for example, in the case of the boy who was possessed with an unclean, deaf and dumb spirit, which the father said entered the boy *as a child* (Mk. 9:17f.). The question put to Jesus by His disciples in John 9:2 when they asked, "Master, who did sin, this man, or his parents, that he was born blind?" indicates the possibility at times of a *prenatal cause* for oppression by Satan. The Apostle Paul in Romans 5:12-14 shows how that all mankind is affected by the curse which fell upon Adam as a result of his transgression.

Finally, it should also be pointed out that there is no such thing as "minor" or "harmless" involvement where the powers of darkness are concerned. Some of the most severely oppressed victims are often those who merely had warts removed by magic charming, or who played with the ouija board "in fun," or who attended some false religious cult or Spiritualist meeting "out of curiosity," or who had their fortune read although they contend that they "never really believed in the genuineness of such things," or who followed the horoscope column in the newspaper each day, although they did not allow it to "affect their lives and decisions." When one enters Satan's domain, for whatever reason, he opens himself to demonic oppression or subjection, and invokes upon himself the curse of God, whose Word clearly declares that they who participate in any form of occultism are an abomination unto Him!

In view of all of this, the reality of Christians being oppressed, the innocent sometimes suffering "passive" oppression, should be apparent. It is a fact which must first be recognized and acknowledged before liberation from these powers of darkness can be considered, for we have found from experience that until the individual who is experiencing oppression is shown the connection between his occult involvement and such oppression and admits its source, he will not be able to exercise sufficient faith to resist and overcome it. But where such acknowledgment is present, liberation of the Name of Jesus Christ is certain.

METHOD OF DELIVERANCE

Wherever there has been occult participation in any form, it is essential that the following procedure be undertaken and carefully followed or *liberation from occult subjection or oppression will not result.* It cannot be overemphasized that those who are occultly oppressed or subjected cannot be fully delivered in the usual manner by mere exorcism of spirits. Those who have allowed themselves to become bound by these dark powers can only be liberated by direct confession of occult sins and renunciation of Satan and his work in their lives. We have seen those needing liberation, who have been prayed for previously for deliverance, sometimes several times without success, set free from Satan's bondage when the correct Scriptural procedure was undertaken. The same procedure is also necessary for those who are "passively" subjected or oppressed, who have never wilfully or actively participated in occultism, but who, nevertheless, suffer affliction from the powers of darkness as a result of their identification and association with others who did, or who were subjected to such occult contacts as children.

1. *Confession of Faith in Christ.*

If the person who needs liberation is already a Christian (as many are), then he needs only to affirm his faith in Christ. Some, however, will have to be led to make such a confession before the way is opened for their deliverance. Occasionally, there will be those who are primarily seeking relief from demonic oppression, but who have no real interest in following Christ. Such individuals cannot be liberated, at least not permanently, for where there is no sincere commitment to Christ there is no permanent basis for resistance to the Enemy's power. On the other hand, there are others who sometimes are *unable* to make such a confession of Christ without help, inasmuch as one characteristic symptom of occult subjection is the inability to make this confession. In such cases, the oppressed person, bound by the powers of darkness, must be led in a confession of faith in Christ by someone who should have them repeat after them a saving confession. Do not be concerned about the sincerity of such a confession in such cases, for if the subjected individual were not in earnest he would not be seeking liberation. Moreover, all the powers of darkness are often brought to bear upon such oppressed individuals in an attempt to prevent just such a confession of faith, which, as they well know, opens the way for liberation from their bondage. Sometimes it will be found that the person is held in such bondage to these evil powers that it will first be necessary to break Satan's hold by calling upon the power of the blood of Jesus before the individual is capable of following another in a confession of faith in Christ.

2. *Confession of Occult Sins.*

All occult involvement must be confessed if liberation is to be realized. The oppressed should name each specific form of participation which can be recalled and confess it to God as sin. The individual should, for example, make a confession similar to the following: "Father, I confess that I have sinned against your Word by consulting a fortuneteller; by attending a seance, or Spiritualist meeting; by inquiring with the ouija board; by having warts or burns removed by magic charming; by following the horoscope, being hypnotized, and divining for water. I confess these practices as sin, as well as anything else of this nature which I may have forgotten, and ask for and accept your forgiveness, in Jesus' Name."

Occasionally, a Christian, suffering oppression and needing deliverance, whose occult involvement dates *before* his conversion to Christ, will ask if it is necessary to confess these practices now that he is a Christian, inasmuch as all his sins were forgiven upon conversion. We should keep in mind, first of all, that the problem under consideration is not concerned with the question of the oppressed individual's salvation, but *the need of deliverance from occult oppression.* Obviously, the Christian seeking deliverance was not set free from Satan's oppression just because he made a confession of faith in Christ, or he would not be seeking liberation from such oppression! Frequently, moreover, these individuals have also had prayer for deliverance and were not set free. Therefore, there must be some hindrance and valid reason why their conversion to Christ and prayer did not result in their liberation. We have found that until occult sins are recognized as the cause and acknowledged, liberation does not come.

One has, in essence, in the case of occult participation, called upon other "gods" (Ex. 20), and has, thereby, opened the door to these oppressing spirits who have access as long as the victim does not *uncover their presence.* The reason for such acknowledgment of occult participation is that one must go back to the place where he opened the door and gave the powers of darkness access and close it at that point. Admission of occult practices is an acknowledgment that the oppressed individual now recognizes such participation as sin in violation of the Scriptures. Proof that such acknowledgment is necessary is seen in the fact that most who are oppressed as a result of occult involvement do not even know that they had violated God's commandments against these practices. Satan resists such admission because acknowledgment of specific occult sins uncovers the presence of the Enemy at the exact point where he has a hold on the victim. Satan hides, as it were, behind one's unconfessed occult practices and keeps him bound. Confession removes this barrier and betrays his presence, thus preparing the way for liberation from his bondage.

While it is true that upon conversion to Christ one's sins are all forgiven, this does not always mean, however, that some of the consequences of those sins may not still be experienced in the present life, as may be seen, for example, in the case of David (2 Sam. 12). If, for instance, one has lived a life of dissipation and sin to such a degree, before conversion, that he is afflicted by the Enemy with disease and sickness as a result, he is not automatically set free from such oppression and cured of these things merely because he made a confession of faith in Christ and was forgiven those sins which caused his ailments. Moreover, if, upon conversion, spirits of infirmity, such as epilepsy, blindness, dumbness, deafness, and so on, do not leave their victims, who many times are innocently oppressed with these afflictions, then there is no Scriptural warrant for thinking that oppressing spirits, resulting from occult involvement, quietly depart when one becomes a Christian.

By stressing the need of an acknowledgment to God of occult practices by Christians who had such involvement before their conversion, we are not suggesting that they were not forgiven all their sins at Calvary, but that they are, by making such admission to God, *now recognizing and acknowledging these occult practices as sin in violation of the Scriptures and the cause of their oppression.* We have found that when Christians are shown the connection between their oppression and previous occult involvement, as well as their violation of the Scriptures by such participation, their acknowledgment of such practices to God opens the way for liberation from oppression.

Obviously, those who have had occult involvement *after* conversion should make a confession similar to that already suggested upon learning of their violation of the Scriptures through their occult participation, just as they would need to confess any sin they might commit as a Christian. However, in those cases where *all* occult involvement was before one's conversion to Christ, we suggest that this individual make an acknowledgment to God of his recognition of these practices, of which he had been guilty, as sin and the cause of his present oppression. Such admission uncovers the presence of the Enemy at the exact place where he has a hold on his victim to oppress him and may be made in a manner similar to the following as preparatory to liberation: "Heavenly Father, I think Thee for now showing me the sinful character of occult practices. I hereby acknowledge that it was my visit to the fortune-teller, inquiring with the ouija board, attending a seance (and so on) in violation of the Scriptures, which opened the door to my oppression and which was the cause of my present problems at the hands of the Enemy. I believe that all my sins are under the blood of Christ, including these which Thou hast now shown me, in Jesus' Name."

One should not allow Satan, through pride or on the basis of theological argument, to hinder him from confession or acknowledgment of occult participation, for the purpose of such admission is to unmask the presence of the Enemy and reveal the point at which he holds his victim in bondage. Refusal of confession simply means that Satan remains concealed, hidden behind the unconfessed sin itself for "he that covereth his sins shall not prosper: but whoso confesseth and forsaketh them shall have mercy" (Prov. 28:13).

3. *Renunciation of Satan and Command to Depart.*

This must be *a direct command to Satan himself* (not a prayer or request) *on the part of the person seeking or needing the deliverance* for Satan to depart in Jesus' Name! No one else can do this for the oppressed or subjected person, inasmuch as it was by an act of this individual's will that the door was opened to the Enemy in the first place, and Satan will, therefore, only heed a command from the same individual to depart, at least permanently. This is another reason why many times those who are occulty subjected or oppressed were not permanently liberated, although others have prayed for them to be delivered. Satan contends, in the case of occult involvement, that he has the "right of access" to this person who has invited him in through occult participation, and that he will not leave until this same individual, by an act of his will, renounces him and commands him to depart. At this point, the oppressed individual should say, for example, "Satan, I hereby renounce you and all your works in my life. I command you in Jesus' Name to depart and trouble me no more! I hereby close the door to you forever."

4. *Exorcism: The Prayer of Deliverance.*

Although we believe, when done in faith, one can liberate himself from occult bondage and oppression by (1) a confession of occult involvement, and (2) a renunciation of Satan, with the command for him to depart, it is, however, advisable to have another exorcise these powers of darkness in those instances where the oppressed individual's faith is weak and the oppression severe. I have found that liberation is usually felt quite definitely by the person who is suffering oppression during this act of exorcism when Satan is commanded to loose the victim and set him free in Jesus' Name. Again and again, a countenance marred by depression as a result of Satanic oppression has been seen transformed at this moment, amid expressions of rejoicing and praise to God at the joy of actually experiencing the dark powers depart. Therefore, in those instances where the hold of demonic power is so tenacious, or one's faith so weak that the oppressed individual cannot break through to liberation without prayer and help from others, one should not hesitate to call upon those who have a sympathetic understanding of the nature of occult oppression and subjection for help.

5. *Responsibility of the Liberated.*

The important thing to remember after deliverance has taken place is that DELIVERANCE IS A WALK, not a once for all experience without any responsibilities on the part of the person who has been set free. After deliverance it is necessary to build certain safeguards around the ground that has been liberated and recovered from the Enemy. Jesus warns in Matthew 12:43-45 that deliverance is not necessarily permanent unless one takes certain spiritual precautions against the Enemy's attempts to return. Thus, if the life of the liberated individual is not filled with faith and spiritually wholesome things, the evil spirit can return bringing with him seven other spirits more wicked than himself and the last state of that individual is worse than the first. Generally, one should avoid all future contact with any form of spiritism or false religious cults. Be on guard against new or strange doctrines that are not in harmony with Scripture. Moreover, one should not neglect to destroy all occult objects and literature (without regard to their cost), such as fortunetelling cards, ouija boards, occult games, magic books, literature from such cults as, for example, Rosicrucians, Christian Science, and Unity, or by such authors as Edgar Cayce, Annalee Skarin, Harold Sherman, and so on (See Acts 19:18-19). It is imperative that one cultivate a strong faith and spiritual life after deliverance. We suggest the following:

(1) *Study of the Scriptures.*

Faith comes by hearing and believing the Word (Rom. 10:17). Strengthen your faith with such passages on deliverance, protection, and the power of Jesus' Name and blood as: Psalm 91; Romans 8:28-39; Revelation 12:11; Luke 10:17; Mark 16:17f.; John 10:27-29; Isaiah 54:11-17, Ephesians 2:6; 6:10f.; Exodus 12:23.

(2) *Prayer.*

Develop a consistent prayer life. Pray much in the spirit. Praying in fellowship with other Biblically sound Christians in a prayer group develops faith and encourages spiritual growth. Prayer partners are recommended. See Luke 18:1; Ephesians 6:18; Jude 20.

(3) *Fellowship.*

Spiritual fellowship with other members of the Body of Christ is essential. A member separated from one's physical body would soon atrophy and die. An ember taken from the fire soon grows cold. Especially does one, who has suffered oppression, need communion with the saints in worship for mutual encouragement, and for spiritual nurture, growth, strength and development. See Hebrews 10:24-25; Acts 2:41-47.

(4) *Resistance.*

After liberation Satan may seek to oppress again, or through temptation attempt to entice the individual to yield to him in order to gain access to his life once more. It is well to remember, therefore, that Satan must have the consent of the individual's will in order to gain an entrance, for we are told in 1 Timothy 4:1, for example, that those who departed from the faith *gave heed* to seducing spirits. We are admonished in Ephesians 4:27 not to "give place to the devil," but to "resist the devil, and he will flee from you" (Jam. 4:7). However, even if the Enemy did break through in a moment of weakness, one should immediately take a firm stand and refuse to give him further access, demanding that he depart.

It would be well to keep in mind the following principles of spiritual warfare in order to maintain one's victory over the powers of darkness and prevent any future invasion of one's life by these malevolent spirits:

a. Confess your victory and deliverance through Jesus' blood (Rev. 12:11).

b. Claim your authority over Satan by virtue of your position with Christ "far above all principality, and power, and might, and dominion" (Eph. 2:6; cf. 1:20-21; Col. 2:13-15; Ps. 91; Mk. 16:17).

c. Use the shield of faith and the sword of the Spirit in time of temptation or assault from the Enemy. Jesus overcame Satan's temptations with Scripture saying: "It is written" (Mt. 4:1f.). Paul admonishes us "above all, take the shield of faith, wherewith ye shall be able to quench all the fiery darts of the wicked one" (Eph. 6:16).

d. Resist Satan in faith, for we are in a spiritual warfare in which we can always have the victory if we will take it by faith (1 Pet. 5:8-9; Mt. 26:41; Jam. 4:7; Eph. 4:27).

e. Put on the whole armor of God (Eph. 6:10-18). This should be done in faith daily, especially in time of great trial.

f. Command Satan to depart in Jesus' Name when he tempts or attacks in any unusual manner, particularly when he seeks to take some advantage of a weakness, or makes an attack through another individual (Mt. 16:21-23, Mk. 16:17; Lk. 10:17).

g. Keep guard over your mind and thoughts. Absolutely refuse entrance into your heart and mind anything of a negative, critical, contrary, resentful, selfish, base, or depressive nature. Guard your mind jealously, for this is where the Enemy usually strikes. Refuse every thought that is impure, unkind, offensive, unjust, evil, detrimental, or envious. Resist and repulse thoughts of pride, hate, resentment, slander, doubt, unbelief, anxiety, indifference, wrath, and self-pity. In so doing the Enemy can gain no access to your life, inasmuch as the greater part of his effort is directed toward making an invasion of your mind. Few people resist him as they should at this point and thus fall prey to his influence and control. Failure to guard the mind and heart against Satan's deceiving, depressive, negative and destructive thoughts and suggestions is one of the major causes for oppression, sickness, fear, discord, depression, despair, strife and failure. "Keep thy heart with all diligence: for out of it are the issues of life" (Prov. 4:23).

The responsibility of the one liberated to keep the door closed to further invasions by the powers of darkness cannot be over-emphasized, for we have seen a few who neglected their responsibility suffer oppression again. This warning should be especially heeded by those neurotic individuals who manifest a spirit of "self-pity" and "self-centeredness" as were described in Chapter 3. These individuals desire attention at any cost. Although it is a morbid and pathological sort of desire for recognition, nevertheless, they feel such a deep-seated need for attention they actually fear (often subconsciously) full deliverance lest they lose the notice of others. Feeling unable to face life, or make independent decisions, and constantly threatened with a specter of failure and misfortune, they do not follow through with their responsibilities and keep the door closed to these dark powers. They constantly lament their fate, confess doubt, fear and failure, voicing their problems and troubles to any and all who will listen. Such are to be firmly admonished concerning their failure to accept their responsibilities, never pitied and sympathized with, since this only feeds this selfish spirit of self-centeredness which thrives on attention and will depart only when it fails to get it. Pray for such individuals, but do not under any circumstances encourage this condition. They must be willing to admit their weakness in this regard, command this spirit to leave, and firmly resist its efforts to return by not encouraging it with their own appetites for attention. There is no cure for the ego-centered person whose liberation from occult enslavement rests entirely in their own wills. They must, if they expect permanent victory, resist any new inroads by this spirit as resolutely as a former alcoholic or drug addict would in taking another drink or injection of narcotics. In all cases, one maintains his position of victory by resistance and faith. Confess victory by faith and stand on it.

In summary, liberation from occult subjection and oppression basically involves *three steps,* which are the essential things to remember in dealing with those who have had any form of occult involvement. They are (1) *Confession of sins of occult participation;* (2) *Renunciation of Satan and the command for him to depart;* and (3) *Exorcism* (when required). In no case have we failed to see a person liberated from the powers of darkness who sincerely desired it and followed these Scriptural requirements.

After prayer for deliverance, accept the fact of your liberation from the powers of darkness *by faith.* Do not rely on "feelings" or "appearances" at this point. Stand on the Word of God—the assurance and evidence will come. At times no change was noted immediately by some of those for whom we have prayed for deliverance, but they later testified to definite liberation from their oppression and subjection to occult powers. Satan knows that he must release his victim when commanded to do so in Jesus' Name, but this does not mean that he always does so immediately, or that certain symptoms disappear at once. Boldly confess the fact of your liberation by faith for the victory is won!

5

DEMONISM TODAY IN THE LIGHT OF SCRIPTURE

In this concluding study, the Biblical basis will be set forth to sustain the fact that there exists an unseen, but nevertheless real, kingdom of darkness, consisting of a complex hierarchy of evil forces, an invisible host of malevolent spirits, all actively engaged in an insidious plot to deceive, control, oppress and eventually destroy the human race. As shown in the foregoing chapters, the basic strategy of Satan, the arch deceiver, is first to gain control of the minds and lives of men and women everywhere by ensnaring them in a demonic web of some form of occultism.

The reality of the existence of these demonic powers is clearly affirmed by the Old Testament itself as seen in the stringent legislation against any traffic in the occult by the Israelites, such involvement being punishable by death (Ex. 22:18; Lev. 20:27). The satanic confederacy and its warfare against the whole creation, beginning with the manifestation of Satan himself at the very inception of the human race (Gen. 3), can be traced throughout the Old and New Testaments. With the Advent of Christ and the establishment of the Church, the conflict between the forces of righteousness and the powers of darkness for control of the created order breaks forth on a scale hitherto unknown, exceeded only by the present demonic flood of wickedness being unleashed against the world how at the consummation of the ages. This is precisely what the Scriptures predict (2 Thess. 2:1-12; 1 Tim. 4:1-3; 2 Tim. 3:1-5; Mt. 24:11, 24; cf. Eph. 6:10-13; 1 Jn. 4:1-3; 2 Jn. 7-11; 2 Cor. 11:13-15; Rev. 13:1f.). Apart from the testimony of the Scriptures, there is no satisfactory explanation for the present-day revival of witchcraft, spiritism and occultism in all forms, nor the alarming increase in war, crimes, suicide, racial strife, social unrest, mental illness, disease, divorce, juvenile delinquency, sexual perversion, adultery, and revolt against law and order.

As was shown in the preceding chapter, the contemporary Church, to a great extent, lives in a world of make-believe with regard to recognition of the extensive influence of deceiving and malevolent spirits working against the human race, being deluded by the unscriptural idea that Satan presents no serious threat to the Christian today. The popular notion is that since Satan was defeated by Christ at Calvary, his present work is largely limited to blinding the eyes of the lost to the truth of the Gospel and harrassing Christians by tempting them with worldly allurements or sinful pleasures. Such a naive attitude has no basis in Scripture whatever. It is significant that the Apostle Paul still calls Satan "the prince of the power of the air" and "the god of this world" *after* Calvary (Eph. 2:2; 2 Cor. 4:4)! The Scriptures warn believers that they should "be sober, be vigilant; because your adversary the devil, as a roaring lion, walketh about, seeking whom he may devour: Whom resist stedfast in the faith" (1 Pet. 5:8-9; cf. Eph. 6:10-13). Satan's invisible hosts are engaged in a ceaseless warfare against believers in an effort to hinder, deceive, discourage, defeat, oppress, maim and destroy.

Moreover, the Church in abandoning its belief in the need of the charismatic gifts today (1 Cor. 12), reasoning that they were merely a kind of temporary foundation in the erection of the first century Church, has at the same time surrendered its charismatic power to cope effectively with the forces of darkness. The Church was called and invested with the necessary power and authority to conduct an effective warfare against the powers of darkness. Casting out demons, binding the forces of evil, and loosing victims from the oppression and bondage of Satan are still as much the duty of the Church as the proclamation of salvation in Christ, and are, in fact, a vital and inseparable part of the Gospel itself which Christ commissioned His Church to preach (Mk. 16: 15-20). As a result of surrendering its charismatic power to heal and deliver from satanic oppression, the pastoral ministry of the Church today is largely limited to "soul-care"; consequently persons suffering mental, physical, or psychic disorders are referred to other professionals for medical or psychotherapeutic treatment. In these areas of human need, the pastor has largely been reduced to a kind of religious psychiatrist trying, through counselling and prayer, to cope with the *effects* of these insidious powers in the lives of men and women, rather than dealing with their *cause*—Satan.

When the Church dissected the commission, separating the Word from the signs which were given to confirm it, it lost the power to convince the unbelieving world, and as a result has been steadily losing ground in country after country to the powers of darkness. Only by a fresh enduement of power from on high and restoration of a charismatic ministry to the Church will it be able to meet and overcome the present-day flood of demonic wickedness sweeping across the earth.

EXISTENCE AND REALITY OF THE KINGDOM OF DARKNESS

For we wrestle not against flesh and blood, but against principalities, against powers, against the rulers of the darkness of this world, against spiritual wickedness in high places (Eph. 6:12).

The Scriptures inform us that God created not only a material or physical world but also an invisible spiritual realm consisting of angels and other spiritual intelligences, such as cherubim (Gen. 3:24; Ezek. 28:14-15), seraphim (Isa. 6:1f.), living creatures (Rev. 4:6f.; 5:1f.), and other unnamed hosts and ministers of God (Pss. 103:20-21; 148:2-5; 84:1). The creation and existence of an invisible, spiritual realm, as well as the visible, is shown by the Apostle Paul in Colossians 1:16: "For by him were all things created, that are in heaven, and that are in earth, visible and invisible, whether they be thrones, or dominions, or principalities, or powers: all things were created by him, and for him" (cf. Neh. 9:6; Ps. 148:2-5).

These invisible hosts, dwelling either in the presence of God or in heavenly regions in close proximity to the earth, are of two orders: the good and the evil. The Scriptures further divide these two orders into a hierarchy consisting of thrones, dominions, principalities, authorities, powers, world rulers, spirit-forces in the heavenlies, angels, archangels, princes, cherubim, seraphim, and other spiritual hosts. Some of the designations refer to holy angelic authority, others denote evil supernatural forces, while some may refer to either, depending upon the context. Certainly, the powers of darkness and the satanic confederacy are under consideration in such passages as Romans 8:38-39, Ephesians 6:12 and Matthew 12:24-26, and doubtless also in Ephesians 1:20-21 (perhaps both in Colossians 1:16 and 2:10).

Satan in Isaiah 14:13 refers to the reality of his kingdom, saying, "I will exalt *my throne* above the stars of God," while Christ Himself acknowledges its existence in Matthew 12:26 saying, "If Satan cast out Satan ... how shall then *his kingdom* stand?" The Apostle Paul speaks of him as "the prince of the power of the air," literally, "the ruler of the authority of the air," or the regions in proximity to the earth, and as "the god of this age." When Satan offered Christ the kingdoms of this world in return for His acknowledgment of Satan as god, Jesus did not challenge his right to offer them, for Christ Himself three times referred to Satan as "the ruler of this world." John designates him as the head of the present world-system (1 Jn. 5:19), ruling in world affairs and directing from his throne in the heavenlies, to whatever extent they yield to his influences, men and governments, as well as educational, social, economic, financial, political, and, in some instances, religious institutions.

ORIGIN OF EVIL: SATAN AND THE DEMONIC POWERS

A perplexing question, and one to which there is no simple solution, concerns the origin of Satan and his host of demonic spirits. Inasmuch as God is not the Author of evil, for the Scriptures show that He created all things good in the beginning (Gen. 1:31), how then could sin originate in a perfect universe, or holy angels and spirits fall into the sin of rebellion against God in the first place? In order to shed light on this mystery, it will first be necessary to examine what God has revealed in His Word concerning Satan, inasmuch as the Scriptures designate him as the father and source of all that is evil.

SATAN

First of all, the Scriptures clearly show that Satan is not some mere impersonal evil "power," or "influence," the "negation of good," but an intelligent, spiritual personality, ruler of a vast kingdom, and god of this world. The Scriptures contain many references to the fact of the personality of Satan: (1) personal pronouns are used in reference to him (Job 1:8; 2:1-2; Mt. 12:26); (2) he possesses intelligence and cunning (Gen. 3:1f.; 2 Cor. 2:11; Eph. 6:11); memory (Mt. 4:6); knowledge and emotions (Rev. 12:12); will (Isa. 14:12f.); speech faculties (Job 1-2; Mt. 4:1f); and (3) he will be punished as a moral, responsible being (Mt. 25:41; Rev. 20:10).

What do the Scriptures reveal as to the origin of Satan, the source of evil? From the fact that the Bible shows that God is the Creator of *all* things, both visible and invisible, whether they be thrones, dominions, principalities or powers (Col. 1:16; Jn. 1:1-3), and that He created all things good (Gen. 1:31), we may conclude that the spiritual being designated Satan in the Scriptures was not originally a fallen creature. Do the Scriptures shed any light on this? We believe that they do. It is highly improbable that this arch enemy of God and man, the source and cause of all the evil and misfortune in the universe, would be unceremoniously introduced into Scripture (Gen. 3) without some revelation in the Word of God as to his origin and subsequent apostasy, as well as some insight into the nature of his kingdom.

There are several passages of Scripture which have reference to Satan's creation, apostasy and fall from his original exalted position in heaven, two of which deserve special consideration; namely, Isaiah 14:1-20 and Ezekiel 28:1-19.[3] What is the true identity of the person described in these passages? A careful study will reveal that the description in these passages cannot be limited to the historic kings of Babylon and Tyre, inasmuch as the language, although addressed to them, evidently goes beyond these kings and characterizes Satan himself.

In the first place, the scope of Isaiah's prophecy is future, looking even beyond Israel's return from the Babylonian exile. Chapter 14:1-3 introduces the time of Israel's Millennial blessings when she is restored to Palestine (14:1), ruling over her oppressors (14:2), and has been granted rest in her own land (14:3). The language in verse 12, which is addressed to the king of Babylon, is also used of Satan (Lk. 10:18; Rev. 12:7-10), who, as the prince of this world, was the directing spiritual influence and power behind the king. Moreover, the language in verses 13-14 is inappropriate if limited to that earthly monarch. There are five "I wills" of Satan in this passage which cannot be applied to the king of Babylon. Satan boasted: "I will ascend into heaven"; "I will exalt my throne above the stars of God"; "I will sit upon the mount of congregation"; "I will asend above the heights of the clouds"; "I will make myself like the Most High." The language, like that in Ezekiel 28:11-19, clearly goes beyond application to the historical king, and is directed to Satan. Ezekiel 28 describes the original, unfallen state of Satan and his apostasy, whereas Isaiah 14 records his fall and ultimate destruction.

Why then are these two prophecies addressed to the historical kings of Babylon and Tyre if they are descriptive of Satan and his career? This is one of the characteristics of divine prophecy and is not uncommon in the Scriptures. Other passages where Satan is addressed indirectly through another are Genesis 3:14-15, Matthew 16:23, and John 13:27. In the Messianic psalms David, while he apparently has reference to himself, in reality describes Christ (cf. Pss. 16:10; 22, etc.). Thus, the kings of Babylon and Tyre have addressed to them language which, by its very nature, seems descriptive of another than themselves. Primarily this is because there is to be seen in the characters and careers of these earthly monarchs the wicked character and career of Satan. Moreover, Satan fulfills himself and his evil administration in and through these earthly kings who rule over his earthly dominions (Lk. 4:5-6), and these rulers, like Satan, arrogated to themselves divine honor and prerogatives (Isa. 14:13-14; Ezek. 28:2).

Next, observe the extraordinary nature of the description in Ezekiel 28:11-19, and the inappropriateness of limiting it to the historic king of Tyre:

"Thou sealest up the sum, full of wisdom, and perfect in beauty" (28:12), that is, one who was complete and perfect before God.

"Thou wast in Eden, the garden of God" (v. 13), not the Eden of Genesis 3, but the paradise of God (v. 14, "the holy mountain of God") where he was arrayed with all imaginable splendor: *"every precious stone was thy covering."*

"In the day that thou wast created" (v. 13). Twice his "creation" is referred to (cf. v. 15), which is inappropriate if applied to the king of Tyre. Of the human race, only Adam is said to have been "created," never his descendants, who are "born."

"Thou wast the anointed cherub that covereth" (v. 14). No satisfactory explanation of the designation "cherub" has ever been offered when applied to the king of Tyre. The cherubim in Scripture are spiritual beings who always appear in the closest relationship to God (Gen. 3:24; Ex. 25:20; 1 Chron. 28:18; Ps. 18:11; Ezek. 1:9-11).

"I set thee, so that thou wast upon the holy mountain of God" (v. 14). He was appointed by God Himself to an exalted position.

"Thou hast walked up and down in the midst of the stones of fire" (v. 14), doubtless signifying the divine presence of God and His glory (cf. 1:17; Ex. 24:10, 17).

"Thou was perfect in thy ways from the day that thou wast created, till unrighteousness was found in thee" (v. 15). Certainly unsuitable and

inappropriate when applied to the king of Tyre who was neither "created" nor "perfect," later falling into a state of unrighteousness. This is, however, an accurate description of the career of Satan. Compare Colossians 1:16 with Ephesians 6:12, and John 1:3 with 8:44 which suggest the fall of Satan from an original state of righteousness. Satan, we are told, "abode not in the truth."

"Thy heart was lifted up because of thy beauty; thou hast corrupted thy wisdom by reason of thy brightness" (v. 17). This is precisely where the Scriptures elsewhere place the cause for Satan's fall and condemnation—pride (1 Tim. 3:6; Isa. 14:13-14).

"Therefore have I cast thee as profane out of the mountain of God; and I have destroyed thee, O covering cherub, from the midst of the stones of fire... I have cast thee to the ground... I have turned thee to ashes... and thou shalt nevermore have any being" (vss. 16-19). This is the exact fate predicted for Satan in Scripture (Rev. 12:7-9; 20:10; Isa. 14:12, 15-20).

In Satan's apostasy and fall he was not alone, for the Scriptures indicate that he was able to persuade numerous angels, and perhaps other spirit beings, to join in his rebellion and attempt to usurp the throne of God. Apparently the angels, possessing moral freedom, underwent a period of probation and testing just as Adam, for we read that some "sinned," and "kept not their first estate, but left their own habitation" (2 Pet. 2:4; Jude 6). The angels of the Devil are referred to in Revelation 12:7. Others who kept their integrity are designated as "holy angels" (Mk. 8:38), and "elect angels" (1 Tim. 5:21). As a result of Satan's rebellion and fall, sin entered the universe which God had created good, polluting it, and Satan became the source of all evil and misfortune (Jn. 8:44). His character and purpose now given over entirely unto evil (he is called a "murderer," "the father of lies," John 8:44, and an incorrigible sinner, 1 John 3:8), he became the Adversary of man, deceiving, oppressing, accusing, and seeking to destroy all that God has created (Gen. 3:1f. Job 1-2; Acts 10:38; Rev. 12:9-10).

The *present realm and sphere* of this Evil One and his hierarchy of wicked powers is not Hell as yet (Mt. 25:41; Rev. 12:7-9), but he is designated as having the seat of his kingdom in the heavenly regions, doubtless in close proximity to the earth (Rev. 12:7-12; Eph. 2:2; 6:12. The "high places" in 6:12 literally mean "heavens" or "heavenly regions"). He walks up and down in the earth at will (Job 1:7; 1 Pet. 5:8), and has access to heaven's throne as the "accuser" of believers (Job 1-2; Zech. 3:1f.; Rev. 12:10). His *present position* is one of royal dignity and authority, so much so that even the archangel Michael "durst not bring against him a railing accusation, but said, 'The Lord rebuke thee'" (Jude 8-9). His *present dominion* is that of king and ruler over a vast kingdom and hierarchy of dark powers (Mt. 12:26, 29; 25:41; Eph. 6:12), being designated as "ruler of this world," "ruler of the power of the air," and having the whole world under his power and influence (Jn. 14:30; Eph. 2:2, 1 Jn. 5:19). As prince of this world, he rules over the godless political systems, in world affairs, in the realm of agnostic science and philosophy, and in the social and economic orders. By his designation as "the god of this world" (2 Cor. 4:4), his *present spiritual and religious power and influence* are signified. His influence and control in religion are to be found in various forms, ranging from subtle perversions of doctrine, including Liberalism, Modernism, and Neoorthodoxy, a recent movement in Protestant thought denying the inerrancy of Scripture, to the revival of witchcraft, false cults, and Devil worship. The worship of Satan and demons is not unknown in Scripture (Lev. 17:7; Dt. 32:16-17; Ps. 106:37; 1 Cor. 10:20; 1 Tim. 4:1f.). Satanic churches are presently in existence, and such things as covenants with the Devil, and prayers to him for assistance have occasionally been disclosed by the oppressed in our counselling with them.

Thus, we see that the Scriptures actually shed much light on the origin of evil in the universe and the present extent and work of the kingdom of Satan. However, the perplexing question yet remains, "How could sin originate in a perfect universe, or holy angels and spirits fall into the sin of apostasy and rebellion against God without outside influence?" Adam transgressed and fell from his state of innocence through the temptations of an outside influence, Satan. But in the case of the transgression of Satan himself, the "anointed cherub" (as well as the holy angels who sinned), there was no one to influence nor tempt him, sin actually having its origin in him, "Thou wast perfect in thy ways from the day that thou wast created, till iniquity was found in thee" (Ezek. 28:15). The Scriptures, while they do not give a direct solution to this profound question, nevertheless, do seem to offer some help in solving this mystery. We offer two suggestions.

1. Satan, angels, and other spirit beings, were, like man, created as *free moral agents*. That is, they were created intelligent, rational, and spiritual, with the power of free moral choice. They were, by God's divine intention, given the power of self-determination with respect to their obedience to God. Obviously, before sin entered the universe, Satan, at that time the anointed cherub, and the angels who later sinned, did not have a choice between good and evil as *realities*, inasmuch as evil as yet did not exist. But evil could exist as a *potentiality* in a universe where God had created other free moral beings to whom he had given the potential power to say "no" to Him and rebel against His will. Before sin entered the universe, there was but one form of transgression possible—the choice between obeying or disobeying God's revealed will and commands. This was the only choice open to Satan initially, as it was later in the case of Adam and his transgression which introduced sin into the world (Gen. 2:16-17; 3:1-6). Irrational beasts do not have this power of choice, nor the right of self-determination, but neither can they, for that matter, worship God and by their own volition serve,

honor, and obey Him. Free response based on love, not forced obedience, would alone satisfy and glorify God, the Father of all creatures, in exactly the same way a parent is honored and pleased by the loving, wilful response and obedience of a child. The initial choice was God's. Irrational beasts or sub-human automatons without the ability of moral choice would present no threat to sanctity of the universe, but God wished to bring into existence beings who could freely worship, honor, and glorify Him. To do this, as God certainly knew beforehand, would require giving them the right of self-determination and the potential power of disobeying Him and His will. A creature who could not wilfully say "no" to God, could not, for exactly the same reason, wilfully say "yes."

Although evil as a reality did not exist from the beginning, it could exist as a potentiality in a free, moral universe, and it is for this reason we are told in John 8:44 that Satan "*abode* not in the truth." We may certainly infer from this that he at one time walked before God in truth and perfection, as Ezekiel 28:15 also indicates, but that he, by an act of his own will, chose not to abide any longer therein. In like manner, many of the angels, with the power of self-determination, "sinned" and "kept not their first estate, but left their own habitation" (2 Pet. 2:4; Jude 6).

2. Satan, angels, and other spirit beings, were, like man, created *finite*. To be "finite" means to be subject to limitations. It is a state of not being perfected (in the absolute sense); it is to be

incomplete. Finiteness stems from the fact of *creation*. It is impossible to create an *infinite* creature—this would be a contradiction. Only god, as uncreated Spirit, without beginning or end, is infinite, i.e., without limitation, but perfect in righteousness, power, wisdom, holiness, and love. Finiteness is inherent in creation. Satan's finiteness was the *door* to his fall, as it was with Adam. If one is finite in his essential nature, then his character, actions, motives, conformity to God's will, power of obedience, and inability to sin, in a word, all that he is and does, will also be subject to this limitation or finiteness. Finiteness in itself does not imply imperfection or defectiveness, but limitation and susceptibility, under certain conditions, to failure or defeat. Satan, as the anointed cherub, was preeminent in beauty and wisdom, possessing many other glorious attributes (Ezek. 28:14). But, being finite, he allowed *pride* to enter his heart because of his beauty ("Thy heart was lifted up because of thy beauty," Ezek. 28:17; 1 Tim. 3:6), as well as *sinful ambition* because of his great position ("I will exalt my throne above the stars of God . . . I will be like the Most High," Isa. 14:13-14). Due to his incomparable beauty and wisdom, and because of his exalted position, his *finiteness* caused him to look away from the truth unto himself—the result was catastrophic—"he abode not in the truth" (Jn. 8:44).

DEMONS

We turn next to the hosts who comprise

Satan's kingdom, demons and fallen angels. [4] Satan, as god of this world, rules over a vast host of demonic spirits and directs an extensive kingdom and hierarchy, consisting of principalities, powers, world rulers of darkness, and spirits of wickedness in the heavenly regions (Eph. 6:12).

In our modern age of science and technology, with the advancements in medical knowledge and psychiatry, and as a result of the rise of critical Biblical scholarship, it has become popular to deny the reality and existence of such personal entities as Satan, demons, and evil spirits, dismissing such belief as unenlightened superstition. Several theories have been proposed by the skeptics in an unsuccessful attempt to explain rationally the manifestation of demonic powers. One such theory contends that the Bible, when it speaks of the presence and activity of demons, merely reflects *prescientific superstition.* From ancient times, we are told, every culture has held to the superstitious belief that the world is inhabited by unseen forces or spirits, some having good intentions toward man and some evil. In this way they were able to explain the mysteries of life and death, accident and disease, prosperity or famine, plagues, floods, storms, and so on. With our present-day knowledge of science and the operation of physical laws, it is no longer necessary to resort to unrealistic explanations based upon unseen spirit forces. Within Christendom some rationalistic theologians propose the *theory of accommodation* in an attempt to explain Jesus' references to demons and His exorcism of the spirits which in some instances possessed those to whom He ministered. Jesus, we are told, in reality was aware that such personal intelligences as demonic spirits did not really exist, but inasmuch as the people to whom He ministered held to these superstitions, He merely accommodated Himself to their unenlightened views concerning the cause of physical and mental illness. His purpose, we are told, was not to teach science, but religion. Hence, He did not attempt to correct their unscientific beliefs. To say the least such a preposterous theory is ethically out of harmony with the moral life and teachings of Jesus Himself as set forth in the New Testament. Others propose the *psychosomatic theory*. So-called cases of demon "possession" were in actuality simply physical or mental disorders. With our present knowledge of medicine and psychiatry many alleged instances of demon activity can now be explained as forms of psychoses or psychoneuroses, habits, addictions, psychological states of the mind, or other physical or mental disorders.

Contrary to such rationalistic explanations, the Scriptures, without reservation, look upon evil spirits, not as mere hallucinations, influences, habits, functional disorders, states of the mind, or psychological problems, but as intelligent personalities. Frequently, behind what may appear to the skeptic to have some logical or natural explanation, Jesus discerned an evil, supernatural entity causing the problem which plagued its human victim. Thus He "rebuked" the fever in Peter's mother-in-law (Lk. 4:39), loosed a woman bowed together by Satan for 18 years by casting out a "spirit of infirmity" (Lk. 13:11-16), and set the "insane" Gadarene free from a legion of demonic spirits (Mk. 5:1f.). Possession by numerous malevolent spirits is not uncommon even in this day as those who have dealt with such oppressed victims can attest, their numbers ranging from a dozen or more to hundreds, and in one instance Satan actually admitting to a pastor through the lips of the victim he possessed that there were 1,067 demons in this individual.

At other times, the Scriptures indicate the reality of the presence of demonic spirits by clearly distinguishing between mere functional disorders and those conditions which result from demonic oppression, for we are told in Mark 1:32-34 that the people brought unto Jesus "... all that were diseased, and them that were possessed with demons ... and he healed many that were sick of divers diseases, and cast out many demons." In Matthew 8:16 disease and demon possession are also distinguished, as they are in Mark 16:17-18, and in Matthew 10:1, where Jesus gave the twelve disciples "power against unclean spirits, to cast them out, and to heal all manner of sickness and all manner of disease." In many instances, however, the Scriptures show that physical and mental oppression are often caused by the presence and activity of evil spirits. In the case of the lunatic child, we read that "Jesus rebuked the demon; and he departed out of him: and the child was *healed* from that very hour" (Mt. 17:14-18). In Acts

10:38 we are told that Jesus *healed* all who were *oppressed of the devil*. Again in Matthew 12:22 the frequent relationship between demon possession and physical affliction is clearly seen: "Then was brought unto him one *possessed with a demon,* blind, and dumb: and he *healed* him, insomuch that the blind and dumb both spake and saw." Demon oppression or possession is never treated merely as an organic disease or functional disorder by Jesus. If caused by an evil spirit, He *cured* the oppressed individual by *casting out the demon.*

Moreover, evidence that Jesus was often dealing, not with mere organic disorders or superstition in the minds of the people, but with distinct intelligences, is to be seen in the Lord's direct commands to the evil spirits (Mk. 5:8); their recognition of Him ("And unclean spirits, when they saw him ... cried, saying, Thou art the Son of God," Mk. 3:11); their display of certain attributes of personality, such as feeling (Mk. 5:7), fear (Lk. 8:31), intelligent speech (Mk. 5:7-12), knowledge (Acts 16:16), as well as their personal names ("My name is Legion," Mk. 5:9). Demons today often identify themselves by name or character as spirits of fear, pride, doubt, lust, resentment, and so on. In our ministry, we have heard demons personally identify themselves either by name or character. In one instance, the demon identified himself, saying, "I am antichrist" (i.e., the spirit of antichrist); another confessed, "I am the demon of death."

The various kinds of evil spirits and the nature

of their work and activity in human life and affairs have already been shown in Chapter 3. There is an almost infinite variety of demonic spirits. There are, for example, spirits of lust, infirmity, insanity, suicide, fear, hate, and pride, as well as deaf, dumb, and blind spirits, who vary in personality, power, appetites, and intelligence. As disembodied spirits, their purpose is to oppress or possess their victims, with the ultimate intention of either the mental, spiritual, or physical destruction of the individual.

HOW DEMONS GAIN ACCESS

How do demonic spirits gain access to their victims to vex, oppress, or possess their minds or bodies? As Matthew 12:43-45 and Mark 5:6-13 clearly indicate, demons as disembodied spirits have no "rest" unless they can find habitation in a physical body, preferably human, through which they can satisfy their own appetites, lusts, and desires. There are basically four avenues which one can open to them whereby they gain access to the mind or body. Counselling interviews with oppressed and afflicted individuals have confirmed this fact.

1. *Emotional crises.*

Not all cases of oppression by evil spirits can be traced to some form of sin or weakness of character on the part of the afflicted individual as is popularly supposed. As a consequence of unusual emotional experiences such as extreme fright, prolonged and abnormal grief over personal loss, or such traumatic and shocking experiences as a child might receive after having witnessed the murder of his parents, or that of a young and beautiful woman who learns that the serious automobile accident in which she was involved necessitated the amputation of both her legs, some individuals have at such times in their state of shock, or fear, actually opened themselves to oppression or invasion by such spirits. In one instance, counselling revealed that the serious emotional and spiritual problems of the person needing deliverance had their inception when the individual was terribly frightened at a very early age. Another who was set free from a spirit causing mental illness, for which he had been institutionalized, traced the cause to a severe emotional crisis which he had experienced just prior to this. Most people do not realize the effect that their attitudes of mind, their fears and doubts, and their negative confessions can have upon them in such times of emotional crisis. A wrong confession, especially at such times when one's body may be weakened by accident or illness, or when in a state of shock, can open the door to the invasion of oppressing spirits. Spirits of infirmity may enter under such conditions, when not resisted, resulting in deformities, chronic conditions, or death. Serious depression and mental illness resulted from harboring guilt feelings since childhood in the case of one individual over the accidental death of a younger member of the family for which she blamed herself. She was later liberated from these oppressing spirits. Such disturbances and afflictions cannot be dismissed merely as psychosomatic disorders, or the result of mental suggestion, but accord well with the teachings of Scripture, for we are told "as a man thinketh in his heart so is he" (Prov. 23:7), that "death and life are in the power of the tongue" (Prov. 18:21), and that we can be "snared" by the words of our mouth (Prov. 6:2). Conversely, a positive confession of the Word of God can bring salvation, healing, blessing and deliverance (Mk. 11:23-24; Rom. 10:10; Ps. 91:2f.; Rev. 12:11, etc.). In another instance, the individual became oppressed by a deceiving spirit who convinced her that she had grievously sinned by submitting to surgery instead of trusting God to heal her. Convinced by Satan that God would not forgive her, she became chronically depressed, suffered psychic oppression, and was bound with a spirit of fear to the point of mental collapse before being liberated.

2. *Sin.*

Such sins as lust, alcohol and drug addiction, theft, sexual excesses, and other sinful habits or forms of intemperance and immorality are frequently the cause of the invasion by unclean spirits in such individuals (cf. Jn. 5:14; Mk. 5:8). One psychically afflicted individual acknowledged during counselling with the author that he actually saw a demon of lust take possession of him as he entered the apartment of his mistress. In another instance, drug addiction resulted in possession by evil spirits from which deliverance was needed. Preoccupation with unclean sexual thoughts and self-abuse by one young man led to total possession by a spirit of insanity and attempts at self-destruction.

Moreover, spiritual transgressions such as prolonged attitudes of hate toward another, or the harboring of resentments, as well as such sins as extreme envy, jealousy, intolerance, pride, uncontrolled anger, lying, desire for revenge, and so on, make such individuals subject to the influence of or invasion by the powers of darkness. This will be evidenced by their exhibiting less and less control over these attitudes and feelings, and by such abnormalities as emotional outbursts, compulsive lying, thoughts of violence and aggression, mental breakdown, depression, unpredictable impulses or behavior, psychic oppression, and other forms of antisocial or psychotic behavior. In more than one situation with which we have dealt, resentments, smoldering beneath the surface for years, have had serious consequences. In two instances women have suffered invasion by spirits causing their physical and mental breakdown as a result of their opposition to, and resentment of, the careers chosen by their husbands. In other cases, hate and resentment led to severe oppression from Satan. Compulsive lying, evidence of the influence of lying spirits in such individuals, has been the consequence in some cases where this weakness was not brought under control. In one instance, a child, who had become a chronic lier, stated that "voices" told her to call the school and create a disturbance by warning them that a bomb was planted in the building. The assassinations of President Kennedy, Robert Kennedy, and Martin Luther King are obvious examples of demonic spirits of hate and intolerance influencing and controlling the perpetrators of these crimes.

3. Doubt, skepticism, and ridicule of divine things.

The possibility of becoming bound by spirits of doubt, deception, and unbelief is far from remote in those careless individuals who persist in negative and skeptical attitudes of mind concerning divine truth, or who resist the ministry and supernatural manifestations of the Holy Spirit today, either through anointed ministers of God or in Spirit-filled believers. King Saul became possessed by an evil spirit as a result of his persistent resistance to God's revealed will, and to David, His anointed servant. The Apostle Paul states plainly that Satan, "the god of this world hath blinded the minds of them which believe not" (2 Cor. 4:4), and that in the last days upon those who do not receive the truth "God shall send them strong delusion, that they should believe a lie: That they all might be damned who believe not the truth, but had pleasure in unrighteousness" (2 Thess. 2:11-12; cf. Mt. 13:10-15; 1 Tim. 4:1-3). It has even occurred in some instances where demons were exorcised from their victims that they immediately entered into those skeptics present who had come to ridicule and criticize. Some adverse effects of demonic influence which result from skepticism and/or ridicule of divine truth are progressive spiritual deterioration, increased resistance to the supernatural and miraculous, religious delusions and doctrinal errors, inner turmoil and anxieties concerning religious matters, and inability to concentrate on the Bible and prayer. In some instances, blasphemous thoughts against Christ, opposition to the Holy Spirit, belligerancy against ministers of the Gospel, and open scorn and ridicule of Christianity in general are the consequences.

4. *Occult involvement.*

The consequences of occult participation or involvement have already been adequately set forth in the preceding chapters. Perhaps more than any other, this is the primary avenue through which the powers of darkness gain access to oppress and afflict their victims, inasmuch as the majority of persons with whom we have counselled either have been involved in some form of occult activity or know of its presence in their family history. The present-day neurosis epidemic, the increase in psychical afflictions and mental and physical disorders, the world-wide chaos, and increasing flood of crime and wickedness are evidence enough of the successful inroads the demonic powers have gained in the lives of men and women everywhere through occult involvement.

THE WORK AND ACTIVITY OF DEMONIC SPIRITS

The purpose at this juncture is to show the activities of the demonic spirits only with reference to their influence and oppression of individuals. We have already indicated the larger scope of the kingdom of darkness and its vast hierarchy of wicked spirits, consisting of thrones, dominions, principalities, powers, rulers of the darkness of this world and spirit-forces in the heavenlies. Scripture designates Satan as head of the present world-system, ruling in world affairs, the satanic confederacy influencing men and nations everywhere, affecting secular and religious institutions alike. With regard to their activity in the lives of individuals, demonic spirits fall into three categories, those which oppress the body, the mind, and the spirit.

1. *Physical infirmities.*

The Gospels contain many references to evil spirits whose primary objective is to afflict their victims with some physical infirmity. These same peculiarities are still in evidence today everywhere.

(1) *Dumb spirits.* A spirit can take possession of, or afflict, some organ of the body, or bind the

nervous center controlling some function. Thus, an evil spirit causing dumbness (a person who is "mute," without the power of speech) paralyzes the speech faculties. In Matthew 9:32-33, we are told that the dumb man possessed a demon and when the demon was cast out by Jesus the dumb man began to speak.

(2) *Deaf spirits.* In this instance, the malevolent spirit binds or afflicts the auditory nerves, resulting in deafness. When both the speech and hearing are affected, the afflicted individual is termed a deaf-mute. Medically, a deaf-mute is one in whom the inability to speak is due to congenital (or early) deafness. However, Jesus treated such a condition as being caused by an evil spirit which He cast out (Mk. 9:25).

(3) *Blind spirits.* The optic nerve, in this instance, is paralyzed by a spirit, in which case it would not have responded to surgery (Mt. 12:22). At times, Satan also afflicts his victims with diseases of the eyes or ears, which, of course, do not always result in blindness or deafness.

(4) *Infirm spirits.* Under this classification is found an infinite variety of oppressing spirits ranging from those which act upon the spinal cord, muscles, or brain, causing such afflictions as deformity, atrophy of the muscles, lameness, and so on (Lk. 13:11f.), to spirits causing asthma, cancer, tumors, heart disease, paralysis, migraine headaches, insomnia, tuberculosis, and such like. Epilepsy, a disease affecting the central nervous system, resulting in severe physical convulsions

and loss of consciousness, may be either an organic affliction or an epileptic spirit. In the latter case, we have found that only by the exorcism of such spirits can the oppressed be set free.

2. *Mental oppression.*

There are spirits whose primary function seems to be to assault the mind with evil or unclean thoughts, feelings of depression, apathy, fear, and anxiety, or with temptations ranging from pride to resignation to failure. There are spirits of insanity who take possession, when possible, of the mental faculties, disrupting normal, rational thought processes, the affected individual exhibiting various mental, emotional, and behavioral abnormalities. Suicide spirits also invade the mind attempting to drive the oppressed individuals to self-destruction or self-injury (Mk. 9:17-22), while others relentlessly press their victims into the performance of some form of shameful or antisocial behavior (Mk. 5:1f.). Other spirits plague their victims with fears, depression, anxiety, feelings of apprehension, panic, or hysteria. Such individuals often become hypersensitive and irritable, or exhibit such destructive emotions as hate, rage, rebellion against authority, resentment, unpredictable moods and impulses, as well as other psychopathic abnormalities (see detailed discussion in Chapter 3 under *Mental and Emotional Disturbances and Abnormalities*).

3. *Spiritual oppression and delusion.*

It is, without doubt, the realm of the spirit in which the forces of darkness are the most aggressive, cunning, and deceptive. Satan's basic strategy is to gain control of the lives of men in order to fulfill his evil purposes through them in his warfare against the kingdom of God. It is for work in this dimension that Satan reserves his most intelligent, cunning, and powerful spirits. One such evil spirit, with the status of "prince" in the satanic hierarchy, was powerful enough to withstand for three weeks a heavenly messenger sent to Daniel, until Michael, the archangel, was dispatched to help him (Dan. 10:1f.). These are of a higher rank, being the "world-rulers of the darkness of this age" (Eph. 6:12), possessing humans and controlling them, whether in the realm of world affairs, or by speaking through Spiritist mediums, or functioning as spirits of divination in fortunetellers and clairvoyants, or influencing false prophets and deluded religious teachers and leaders. The importance of insight into Satan's strategy and methods of operation in the area of the spirit cannot be overemphasized, and is, therefore, the main thrust of this book. The believer is admonished to "put on the whole armor of God, that ye may be able to stand against the *wiles* of the devil."

The activities of these spirits are frequently cloaked with respectability and as *religious seducing spirits* often appear in clerical or religious garb as "an angel of light," or as "ministers of righteousness" (2 Cor. 11:14-15), in the churches, seminaries, and other religious organizations and institutions. As religious spirits they lure the gullible into false cults, or modernistic churches and schools, deceiving them into embracing such religious aberrations as heretical doctrines, denial of the inerrancy of Scripture, legalism, false revelations, and many forms of religious delusion and practice.

With the revival of witchcraft and the worldwide interest in occult and psychic phenomena, seducing spirits are taking advantage of this opportunity to deceive and ensnare the unwary in all forms of occultism, often clothing it with a religious aura of respectability, as may be seen, for example, in Spiritualism, or the increasing use of ESP, spirit healing, and the seance in connection with religious services. Also functioning in this sphere will be found lying spirits whose primary purpose is to seduce and deceive their victims, as well as to induce them to lie or deceive others (1 Kgs. 22:19-23; Acts 5:1f.). In 1 John 4:1, we are warned not to believe every spirit in the sphere of religion, but to test them. Lying and deceiving spirits are predicted as being especially active at the close of the present age, and are, in fact, already going forth in this hour to seduce and deceive (2 Thess. 2:10-12; 1 Tim. 4:1-3, Mt. 24:11, 24).

Again, these spirits often appear in intellectual and cultural garb in the educational, social, cultural, and political realms of world affairs. These are the *spirits of intellectualism, pride, aggrandizement, and avariciousness or greed,* and have far greater influence upon world affairs than most people are aware. Many of the outstanding personalities in these fields, both past and present, have been influenced or directed by such spirits, or have participated in some form of occultism, whereby they subjected themselves to the possibility of such influence by seducing spirits. Some of the world's leading poets, novelists, philosophers, musicians, scientists, and political and religious leaders, often by their own admission, have been interested or involved in some form of occultism and the psychic realm.

The noted philosopher, Socrates, openly acknowledged that he was guided and inspired by his "Daemon" (demon). Dr. Carl Jung, world renowned psychiatrist, was possessed with psychic powers and had many psychic experiences. He had, according to Dr. Nandor Fodor, the well-known psychoanalyst, a spirit-guide, named Philemon, with whom he conversed. He often had horoscopes cast for his patients, and his doctoral thesis was on the subject of occult phenomena. Thomas Edison's parents were Spiritualists who conducted seances in their home. Mary Baker Eddy, the founder of Christian Science, is said to have worked as a professional medium in New York, and Joseph Smith, founder of Mormonism, received his "revelations" from a discarnate spirit named Moroni. Emanuel Swedenborg, scientist-theologian, whose followers founded the Churches of the New Jerusalem based on his teachings, reportedly communicated with the "dead" on frequent occasions.

It is common knowledge that seances were held in the White House during the presidency of Abraham Lincoln, and some writers contend that the records show that one major decision at least was influenced by these spirits speaking through the mediums; namely, the Emancipation Proclamation! Lincoln's apparition has reportedly been seen in the White House by others (a common phenomenon in houses where seances have been held), the most notable being Queen Wilhelmina of Holland during the presidency of Franklin D. Roosevelt. According to the psychic medium, Jeane Dixon, she was invited on more than one occasion by the late President Roosevelt, whose death she predicted, to the White House for consultation. Woodrow Wilson is also said to have consulted mediums for guidance during the First World War. MacKenzie King, former Prime Minister of Canada, is said to have been actively engaged in Spiritualism and sought spirit guidance in affairs of state, according to Fred Archer, noted writer on spiritualism and psychical research. He also reports that Sir Winston Churchill acknowledged that he had, at times, used the planchette and had done automatic or spirit writing. The psychical interests of Britain's Queen Victoria, as well as that of W. E. Gladstone, Prime Minister of England in the nineteenth century, were such that they attended seances and sought communication with the dead. Furthermore, Archer in his book, *Exploring the Psychic World*, contends that records indicate that the British Royal Family has had some contact with spiritualism for over a century, and that King George of Greece was an active Spiritualist.

Arthur Ford, a Disciples of Christ minister and psychic medium who conducted the seance in which the late Bishop James A. Pike allegedly communicated with his dead son, states in his book, *Nothing So Strange,* that many notable personalities have consulted him, for whom he has conducted seances. He claims to have given sittings for many important persons in government circles—generals, admirals, ambassadors, congressmen, senators, and members of the State Department. Through the *Spiritual Frontiers Fellowship,* which he founded, many churchmen have become involved in psychic matters, and occultism has made inroads into churches of various denominations, as well as other religious organizations. As with Jeane Dixon, Ford's psychic powers have brought him invitations for consultations and demonstrations far and wide. He states, for example, that he has conducted seances in the Hyde Park Methodist Church of Chicago, in addition to many others, held seances for Upton Sinclair, American novelist, Dr. Sherwood Eddy, founder of the YMCA in the Orient, Ruth Montgomery, author of *A Gift to Prophecy* (Jeane Dixon), Glenn Clark, founder of CFO, Dr. Ozora Davis, former president of Chicago Theological Seminary, and demonstrated his psychic abilities before the committee appointed by the Archbishop of Canterbury several years ago to inquire into the claims of spiritualism.

There has been such a phenomenal revival of interest in astrology that *Time* magazine featured the subject in its March, 1969 issue. In the United States alone there are thousands of astrologers, either full or part-time, who chart the heavens for millions of interested followers. *Time* lists among those who have shown interest in this ancient occult method of divination in America such personages as J. P. Morgan, Caruso, Mary Pickford, Robert Cummings, Marlene Dietrich, Peter Lawford and Ronald Reagan, now Governor of California.

Astrologers were engaged by several governments during World War II who produced astrological calculations for propaganda purposes; in addition they made predictions as to the enemy's tactics and the outcome of the war. Horoscopes were cast for all the Allied and Axis leaders and exhaustively analyzed. In Nazi Germany, Himmler employed a corps of clairvoyants and astrologers, while the astrologer Louis de Wohl claims to have functioned in this capacity for the British government. The Russians also seem to have had an astrologer who served under Stalin and Krushchev.

In the literary field, Conan Doyle, well known British author of detective mysteries (Sherlock Holmes), was active in spiritualism and also its avid defender. Charles Dickens, who seems to have had certain psychic experiences, once confided that every word uttered by his characters in his novels was distinctly heard by him as spirit voices before being written down. According to writers on the occult, Henry Wadsworth Longfellow, the American poet, was interested in psychic phenomena and attended seances, and Lord Tennyson and John Ruskin shared interest in the psychic field. Harriet Beecher Stowe, who, it is said, was psychic from childhood, stated that she did not really write *Uncle Tom's Cabin* but that it came to her in vision. Samuel Clemens (Mark Twain), American author and humorist, was a member of the (occult) Society for Psychical Research, and reported his own psychic experiences.

Certainly, horror fiction, with its monsters, vampires, werewolves, ghosts, murders, and gruesome and revolting subject matter, would seem to indicate inspiration from occult sources. Such novels as *Frankenstein, Dracula, Dr. Jekyll and Mr. Hyde,* as well as the horror fiction of Edgar Allan Poe, Washington Irving, Nathaniel Hawthorne, Goethe, and Charles Dickens suggest this. As we know, the works of Shakespeare are replete with witches, ghosts, magic, blood and murder. Current interest in the occult in the literary field is reflected in the immense increase in the sale of occult literature, the abundance of horror movies, the plays and television programs which reflect occult influence, as well as the popularity of monster and horror comics for children. The bizarre, strange, macabre and demonic seem to have captivated the minds of young and old alike, and it is not difficult to show that there exists a high coincidence between this fascination with the occult and the increase in physical, emotional, and psychic disturbances today.

[1] Psychic "gifts" and powers resulting from occult involvement are not to be confused with genuine gifts of the Holy Spirit, authentic visions, and other divine, supernatural phenomena, which do have a vital place in the life of the believer and the Church (e.g., Mark 16:17f.; 1 Cor. 12:1f.; Acts 1:16f);

[2] Thus proving beyond question that dowsing has nothing to do with so-called "magnetic" forces attracting the rods as some allege, inasmuch as it is also effective when used over a map of the site. Its source is demonic.

[3] For a more detailed study of this question, see the author's book, *An Introduction to the Old Testament Prophets* (Moody Press), pp. 304-308.

[4] We distinguish between demons and fallen angels as the two terms seem never to be equated nor used interchangeably in Scripture. No angel is ever said to be "in" a person as in the case of the demon possessed. We do not, for example, read of a person being possessed by an "unclean angel" (e.g., Lk. 4:33-36). Moreover, angels and other spirits are distinguished in Acts 23:9. As we have already shown, the Scriptures speak of many kinds of spiritual creatures.

— NOTES —

— NOTES —

— NOTES —

— NOTES —